Series Editors:
Dario Castiglione (University of Exeter) and
Vincent Hoffmann-Martinot (Sciences Po Bordeaux)

the personalisation of politics

a study of parliamentary democracies

Lauri Karvonen

First published by the ECPR Press in 2010

The ECPR Press is the publishing imprint of the European Consortium for Political Research (ECPR), a scholarly association, which supports and encourages the training, research and cross-national cooperation of political scientists in institutions throughout Europe and beyond. The ECPR's Central Services are located at the University of Essex, Wivenhoe Park, Colchester, CO4 3SQ, UK

Typeset by the ECPR Press
Printed and bound by Lightning Source

British Library Cataloguing in Publication Data
A catalogue record for this book is available from the British Library

Paperback ISBN: 978-1-9073010-3-2

Hardback ISBN: 978-1-9073011-1-7

www.ecprnet.eu/ecprpress

Publications from the ECPR Press

ECPR Classics:

Identity, Competition and Electoral Availability: The Stabilisation of European Electorates 1885–1985 (ISBN: 978-0-9552488-3-2) Stefano Bartolini and Peter Mair

People, States and Fear: An Agenda for International Security Studies in the Post-Cold War Era (ISBN: 978-0-9552488-1-8) Barry Buzan

Elite and Specialized Interviewing (ISBN: 978-0-9547966-7-9) Lewis A. Dexter

System and Process in International Politics (ISBN: 978-0-9547966-2-4) Morton A. Kaplan

Democracy (ISBN: 978-0-9552488-0-1) Jack Lively

Individualism (ISBN: 978-0-9547966-6-2) Steven Lukes

Political Elites (ISBN: 978-0-9547966-0-0) Geraint Parry

Parties and Party Systems: A Framework for Analysis (ISBN: 978-0-9547966-1-7) Giovanni Sartori

Electoral Change: Responses to Evolving Social and Attitudinal Structures in Western Countries (ISBN: 978-0-9558203-1-1) Mark Franklin *et al*

Citizens, Elections, Parties: Approaches to the Comparative Study of the Processes of Development (ISBN: 978-0-9552488-8-7) Stein Rokkan

ECPR Monographs:

The Return of the State of War: A Theoretical Analysis of Operation Iraqi Freedom (ISBN: 978-0-9552488-5-6) Dario Battistella

Gender and the Vote in Britain: Beyond the Gender Gap? (ISBN: 978-0-9547966-9-3) Rosie Campbell

Paying for Democracy: Political Finance and State Funding for Parties (ISBN: 978-0-9547966-3-1) Kevin Casas-Zamora

The Politics of Income Taxation: A Comparative Analysis (ISBN: 978-0-9547966-8-6) Steffen Ganghof

Joining Political Organisations: Institutions, Mobilisation and Participation in Western Democracies (ISBN: 978-0-9552488-9-4) Laura Morales

Citizenship: The History of an Idea (ISBN: 978-0-9547966-5-5) Paul Magnette

Representing Women? Female Legislators in West European Parliaments (ISBN: 978-0-9547966-4-8) Mercedes Mateo Diaz

Deliberation Behind the Closed Doors: Transparency and Lobbying in the European Union (ISBN: 978-0-9552488-4-9) Daniel Naurin

Globalisation: An Overview (ISBN: 978-0-9552488-2-5) Danilo Zolo

General Interest Books:

Parties and Elections in New European Democracies (ISBN: 978-0-9558203-2-8) Richard Rose and Neil Munro

Masters of Political Science (ISBN: 978-0-9558203-3-5) Edited by Donatella Campus and Gianfranco Pasquino

Please visit www.ecprnet.eu/ecprpress for up-to-date information about new publications.

contents

list of figures and tables

FIGURES

Chapter 4

TABLES

Introduction

Chapter 1

Chapter 2

acknowledgements

An exhaustive list of the individuals and institutions that have supported me would be too long to be included in this short preface. Some individuals must nevertheless be singled out, as their assistance has been essential for the success of my work.

'Democracy: A Citizen Perspective. An Interdisciplinary Centre of Excellence' (D:CE) at Åbo Akademi University has provided a research environment of an ideal kind. Of my D:CE colleagues, I must record my special thanks to Tom Carlson. Without Tom's help and advice, it would have taken me much longer both to get started and to complete this process. Åsa Bengtsson, Göran Djupsund, Kimmo Grönlund and Peter Söderlund have in various ways contributed to the process; my heartfelt thanks to all of you.

The research programme on 'Power in Finland' (VALTA) of the Academy of Finland provided a grant for the project called 'Citizen Power in Representative Democracy' (No. 117814) of which this study is a part. A personal research grant from the Finnish Society of Sciences and Letters has also contributed to the positive conditions surrounding my work.

Åbo, Hus Lindman,
Lauri Karvonen

1 introduction

Several generations of scholars have argued that the importance of the structural and ideological foundations of politics in the Western world is in decline. When Daniel Bell in 1960 proclaimed the end of ideology in his analysis of American politics in the 1950s, he spoke of 'a decade marked by extraordinary changes in the class structure, particularly in the growth of the white-collar class and the spread of suburbia' (p. 13). Just five years later, Otto Kirchheimer very much echoed the gist of Bell's reasoning when coining another catchphrase: 'Under present conditions of spreading secular and mass-consumer goods orientation, with shifting and less obtrusive class lines, the former class-mass parties and denominational mass parties are both under pressure to become *catch-all peoples' parties*' (1966: 190, my emphasis). The work published by Ronald Inglehart ever since the early 1970s (1971, 1977, 1990 and 2007) has told us that 'postmaterialist values' are increasingly replacing material concerns as a basis for social and political life.

All of this has had profound effects on the way political scientists view the relationship between citizens and political parties. Although to a large extent organised according to structural cleavages among the population, parties can no longer rely on a stable support provided by economically – or culturally – defined population segments. Political choice is no longer viewed as a mechanical translation of the socio-economic characteristics of the voter. Voters increasingly feel free to make a real choice, and this has permanently affected the mass base of party support. Electoral volatility is increasing as voters feel less and less bound by earlier voting decisions when casting their ballots. While James Bryce's words 'parties are inevitable' (Dalton and Wattenberg 2002: 3) may still be true, most political scientists would probably agree that there is an ongoing 'decline of parties' (Webb 2002: 2).

If 'class' is increasingly less important as a determinant of party choice and political behaviour, what has come in its stead? Clearly, focus on individual issues has been strengthened. Some questions emerge as central issues in connection with a specific election, and voter choices are strongly affected by how they view these issues and how the parties position themselves on these central questions. The election campaign as a phenomenon has become increasingly important. What happens during the campaign is often decisive for the outcome of the election as a growing proportion of the electorate make up their minds at a very late stage of the campaign (Schmitt-Becker and Farrell 2002: 2–5).

A growing research literature points to another prominent feature of contemporary politics that can be seen as a consequence of the structural transformation of Western societies: *personalisation of politics*. With the transformation and weakening of fundamental social structures, forces other than collective loyalties and identities have increasingly come to condition the political behaviour and preferences of citizens. One of the factors that has gained in importance is the role of individual politicians and of politicians as individuals in determining how people view politics and how they express their political preferences. In a highly-acclaimed book on representative democracy, Bernard Manin (1997: 219) puts it thus:

> [P]eople vote differently from one election to another, depending on the particular persons competing for their vote. Voters tend increasingly to vote for a person and no longer for a party or a platform. This phenomenon marks a departure from what was considered normal voting behavior under representative democracy, creating an impression of a crisis in representation...
>
> Although the growing importance of personal factors can also be seen in the relationship between each representative and his constituency, it is most perceptible at the national level, in the relationship between the executive and the electorate. Analysts have long observed that there is a tendency towards the personalization of power in democratic countries.

Writing about media and political campaigns, Swanson and Mancini (1996b: 10) very much echo this view:

> The growing tendency to aggregate around individual politicians produces a personalization of politics reflecting the atomization of power, which breaks up into many competing centers that conflict and cooperate with each other and seek a political authority, exercised and personified by a single individual, with which to identify. These changes are part of a circular process in which power flows from the party structure, the traditional intermediary of political consensus, to individual politicians, resulting in a lessening of the ability of parties to manage political institutions and, in turn, a decline of the institutions' ability to act effectively.

This book is about this alleged personalisation of politics in advanced Western democracies. The view represented by the quotations above – throughout this book, it will be generically referred to as *the personalisation thesis* – is not taken for granted. Rather, the central aim is to provide a comprehensive answer to the question whether it is accurate and reasonable to speak of a clearly increased and ongoing personalisation of politics in recent decades. By both systematising previous empirical research and presenting new primary evidence this book hopes to provide a more substantiated picture of this important aspect of political development.

FOCUS AND SCOPE

While most authors would argue that the personalisation of politics is a typical feature of contemporary democracies, the phenomenon itself is anything but new. Quite the contrary: in his studies of the historical development of social and political orders, Max Weber identified 'charismatic authority' as one of the three main forms of political legitimacy (1957). Moreover, studies of the early phases of representative democracy have emphasised that political representation largely centred on local notables rather than nationally-identifiable collective interests and loyalties (Manin 1997: 202–3). In fact, it may very well be argued that politics in its pre-democratic forms was much more personalised than it is today.

This book, however, has no ambition to cover possible cases of political personalisation before the establishment of mass-based representative democracy. Those who point to an increased personalisation of contemporary politics naturally do not use these broad historical perspectives as points of comparison. Rather, the argument is based on a comparison with the heyday of class-based, collective political organisation. The industrial society, that peaked approximately half a century ago in the West, was characterised by parties based on the divisions between clearly identifiable socio-economic or cultural groups in society. Parties and ideologies were an expression of the perceived interests of these social segments and political identities; preferences and choices were largely a function of citizens' affiliation to such groups (Mair 2006: 371–4). With the transformation and weakening of these fundamental social structures, forces other than collective loyalties and identities have increasingly come to condition the political behaviour and preferences of citizens. The temporal focus of this book is primarily on the post-industrial period, roughly the decades after the 1970s.

In a similar vein, newer democracies, among which numerous cases of highly personalised politics can surely be identified, fall outside the scope of the present study. For instance, the former communist states in Europe never produced the kind of cleavage-based party system which forms the ideal-typical point of comparison for the personalisation thesis (Gallagher *et al* 2001: 439–46; Lindström 2001: 216–19). The same is true for basically all Latin American countries as well as for those democracies that have emerged in the third world. Ethnocentric or not, it seems reasonable to limit the geographical focus of the study to those Western countries that have been liberal democracies at least since the mid-1970s.

In fact, not even all cases of stable Western democracy can be viewed as equally relevant to this account. At its core, the personalisation hypothesis is primarily based on a notion about parliamentary democracy with its traditional emphasis on the role of collective identities and cohesive political parties (Bowler *et al* 1999: 3–18). Although not immune to the same forces of change that have affected parliamentary systems, presidential democracies have due to their nature always placed a stronger emphasis on individual leaders and candidates. Thus, evidence of personalisation from presidential systems, although by no means irrelevant to the purposes of this study, does not constitute as strong a proof in favour of the personalisation hypothesis as similar evidence in parliamentary systems. The institutional focus of this study is on those democracies where the parliamentary mechanism is an important feature of the political system.

Another limitation in the scope of this study concerns its theoretical level of ambition. It does not purport to test the ultimate question about personalisation, that is, why personalisation has appeared in the first place. The general causal background of personalisation as depicted in the previous literature is taken as a point of departure rather than tested empirically. Overall, much of the empirical evidence presented in this book aims at answers of a basically descriptive kind. Has personalisation indeed increased during recent decades? What is the magnitude of this change? What variations are there in this regard among countries and institutional environments? Is personalisation a linear process? Despite this largely descriptive ambition, it nevertheless seems appropriate to discuss the causal background of personalisation in a concise manner.

WHY PERSONALISATION?

In general terms, the personalisation of politics may be viewed as part of an overall process of individualisation of social life (Bauman 2001). People perceive themselves and others primarily to be individuals rather than as representatives of collectivities and groups. Swanson and Mancini see the personalisation of politics as a result of another overarching development pattern in Western societies: socio-economic and technological *modernisation*. The changes that the media sector has undergone due to technological change are, in their view, essential for understanding the rise to prominence of individual politicians at the expense of parties and institutions (1996b: 7–18).

Moreover, most authors addressing the question of the personalisation of politics point to two more specific developments that form the causal background of personalisation. The pervasive changes in social structures, brought about by economic and technological changes, have led to a process of dealignment vis-à-vis traditional political and social organisations. As these organisations reflect structural cleavages with which the citizens can no longer identify, the result is that citizens' loyalty to those parties and ideologies that represent these cleavages has been weakened. Instead, citizens increasingly focus on specific issues and on individual political leaders and candidates (Dalton *et al* 2002: 37–56).

Parallel to this structural change, the media have definitely become the dominant channel of political information and propaganda. The logic of the media favours persons over abstract issues and interests. Of crucial importance is the central role of television. More than printed media, television automatically focuses on persons and personalities: '…television turns faces into arguments' (Hart 1999: 34). The predominance of television has forced parties to select leaders and candidates who make a favourable impression on television, and this focus on individual politicians has in turn strongly conditioned the way citizens view politics (Farrell 1996: 173–5). Having lasted nearly half a century, the predominance of television as the central forum for politics shows few signs of weakening. The advent of new communications technology has at least not slowed down the process of personalisation; in fact, it may have accelerated it.

WHAT IS PERSONALISATION?

The core of the personalisation hypothesis is the notion that individual political actors have become more prominent at the expense of parties and collective identities. The central concept denotes a process of change over time: at t politics was less personalised than at $t+1$. This process can entail changes in a number of respects. Most of these are closely interrelated, but they do not all need to occur in tandem, and no definite causal hierarchy or temporal sequence need be posited between them. In concrete terms, personalisation of politics may, for instance, entail the following changes (Rahat and Sheafer 2007: 66–8; McAllister 2007: 571–85; Kaase 1994: 212–13):[1]

- Institutions may stress individual politicians over collectivities more than in the past. Changes in electoral systems, nomination rules and the position and powers of individual representatives and office-holders may give individual politicians a sharper profile and more personal leeway than was the case in earlier times;
- The way politics is presented to the citizens may stress the role of individual politicians. Electoral campaigns and political propaganda may centre increasingly on individual candidates and leaders instead of parties, their platforms and the collective interests that they claim to represent. The focus of the mass media may similarly shift to individual politicians and their characteristics and qualities;
- People may increasingly perceive of politics as a competition between individual politicians and leaders rather than organised collective interests;
- People may increasingly form their political preferences on the basis of their images of individual political actors;
- People may increasingly make their political choices based on preferences formed on the basis of their evaluations of individual politicians;
- The choices citizens make on the basis of their evaluations of individual candidates and leaders may decide the outcome of elections;
- Ultimately, power relationships in politics and society may come to be decided on the basis of the individual characteristics of politicians.

In sum, personalisation is a potentially pervasive phenomenon that may affect large parts of the political process. A comprehensive empirical study should therefore embrace several of the above-mentioned aspects.

TAKING STOCK OF RESEARCH

Empirical studies carrying the word 'personalisation' in their titles started to appear in the 1990s. Today, a fairly large body of research has addressed the issue, although no clearly recognisable standard volume seems to have appeared yet. For the purposes of this introduction, a survey of available literature with at least a minimum of longitudinal analysis was carried out. The literature was grouped into three parts. This classification is far from perfect; the studies belonging to the three groups overlap to a considerable extent. Still, one can distinguish two areas where research is clearly focused plus a number of additional studies that address various issues relevant to personalisation:

1   In political psychology, there is a use of 'personalisation' that focuses on the individual citizen. The idea is that the personality traits of citizens have become more important at the expense of their socio-economic features when citizens form opinions on parties, candidates and political issues (see Caprara 2007). Personalisation in this sense falls outside the scope of the present study.

- *Studies of 'presidentialisation'.* These are studies where the core concern is the ever more predominant role of prime ministers in parliamentary systems, although these studies frequently cover a fairly large range of empirical phenomena.
- *Studies of party leader effects in elections.* This is the most clearly focused part of the research where focus is on the difference that voters' evaluations of party leaders may make for the electoral success of parties.
- *Studies with varying empirical foci.* This residual category contains studies that address various aspects of personalisation without clearly forming a coherent body of literature in the same way as the two other categories.

Presidentialisation

The studies addressing the question of presidentialisation stem from two important books. Anthony Mughan's monograph on the British case (2000) has a twin focus on the media coverage of party leaders and the effects of leader evaluations on election outcomes. Using these empirical analyses as a starting point, he then presents a thorough discussion about the causes and effects of presidentialisation. The rest of the studies listed in Table I.1 are included in a volume edited by Thomas Poguntke and Paul Webb, 'The Presidentialization of Politics. A Comparative Study of Modern Democracies' (2005). This is the most ambitious study of presidentialisation thus far. Chapter 1, written by the editors, presents a comparative framework which identifies three 'faces' of presidentialisation: the executive face, the party face and the electoral face. Thirteen empirical chapters present empirical analyses of individual countries[2] structured according to the common analytical framework. The concluding chapter, also written by the editors, offers a substantial comparative summary of the findings in terms of the analytical framework.

Table I.1 summarises the studies on presidentialisation in terms of focus, empirical base and main results. It omits those country analyses included in Poguntke and Webb where the main focus is not clearly on the presidentialisation of parliamentary systems. As was mentioned earlier, the conditions for personalised politics are quite different in systems with a strong president independent of the will of the legislature. In fact, one might ask why the editors have chosen to include a case such the United States at all.

Mughan's study of Great Britain clearly points to an increased presidentialisation of politics, although a clear-cut linear development cannot be discerned. He nevertheless concludes that 'presidentialism would appear to be a characteristic of modern parliamentary elections that is unlikely to go away, largely because political parties have become more dependent in their communications with voters on the essentially visual and personality-based medium of television' (2000: 129). Mughan's analysis is supported by Heffernan and Webb's study five years later, except for their analysis of leader effects on voter choice, where the authors detect only "modest direct significance" (2005: 56). The rest of the studies in the

---

2   Belgium and the Netherlands are analysed in the same chapter

Table 1.1: Studies of 'presidentialisation'. Summary of main contents

Author	Focus	Empirical base	Results	Comments
Mughan 2000	– Media focus on party leader – Leader effects on elections	Britain 1951–1997: – Newspaper mentions of party leaders 1951–97 – TV exposure of party leaders 1964–97 – Survey data on electoral impact of party leaders 1964–97	– '…elections have become more presidential since 1964, and especially in the 1980 and 1990s' (p.51) – '…leader effects …not fixed and have gone up as well as down' (Ibid)	
Heffernan and Webb 2005	– 'Executive face': more leeway to prime minister – 'Party face': shift in intra–party power to the benefit of the leader – 'Electoral face': a) growing leadership appeals in electioneering; b) growing leader focus in media; c) growing leader effects on voting	Secondary sources on British politics	– Growing leader role in governing and electioneering – More leader–centred campaigns, more focus on leaders in media – Leaders 'more strongly placed to exert intra–party power' (p.56) – '… modest direct significance for voter choice' (Ibid.)	Little systematic longitudinal hard evidence

(Contd.)

Table 1.1: Studies of 'presidentialisation'. Summary of main contents (Contd.)

Author	Focus	Empirical base	Results	Comments
Poguntke 2005	– " –	Secondary sources on German politics	– While it is 'likely that the influence of candidate effects… [has] grown… longitudinal analyses are inconclusive' (p. 80) – More mediatisation, a more elevated role for the chancellor – '…does not mean… a linear trend towards growing presidentialization…' (p.81)	Not an unambiguous picture!
Calise 2005	– " –	Secondary sources on Italian politics	– 'The combination of the new electoral law, a strengthened executive and a heavily mediatized political arena produced a majoritarian form of politics' (p. 102)	Little systematic longitudinal hard evidence

(Contd.)

Table 1.1: Studies of 'presidentialisation'. Summary of main contents (Contd.)

Author	Focus	Empirical base	Results	Comments
Fiers and Krouwel 2005	– " –	Secondary sources on Belgian and Dutch politics	– In Belgium '…higher share of preference voters for party leaders' (p. 146), in the Netherlands, '…similar… even though hard data on preference voting are lacking' (p. 147) – Both: '… position of … prime minister has been strengthened significantly' (p. 150)	Limited comparative hard evidence
Bakvis and Wolinetz 2005	– " –	Secondary sources on Canadian politics	– No leader effects over time – 'Campaign… based in good part on… leader' (p. 216) – '… personalization.. of party leadership… evidence somewhat ambiguous' (Ibid.)	Fairly weak evidence of personalisation
Paloheimo 2005	– " –	– Finnish national election studies 1991, 1999, 2003 – Voter Barometers 1975–2003 – Editorials and front pages of the largest Finnish daily 1967–2003	– From 1995 on, statistically significant but rather weak leadership effects on party choice – Increasing media mentions of prime minister	One of the more substantial accounts

volume, edited by Poguntke and Webb, also present sufficient evidence to enable the editors to conclude in the following way: 'Overall, this review suggests that the overwhelming weight of evidence lies in favour of the presidentialization thesis' (Webb and Poguntke 2005: 346).

In the light of a close scrutiny of the relevant chapters in the Poguntke and Webb volume, this seems like rather a strong conclusion. To begin with, although the country chapters follow the common analytical framework developed by the editors, they are not based on identical empirical datasets. In fact, save for Paloheimo's chapter on Finland, they predominantly rely on secondary sources, at times bordering on the anecdotal. While there is no reason to doubt the expertise of the authors, their conclusions are not based on comparable empirical efforts either in terms of time, scope or focus. Moreover, although most authors lean towards supporting the presidentialisation thesis, the overall impression is by no means unambiguous, and the lack of systematic evidence is in several cases problematic. Notably, Germany presents a case where a definite trend cannot be discerned (Poguntke 2005: 80–1).

Party leader effects on voters
Several important studies have addressed the question of party-leader effects on voter choice and electoral outcomes. In an impressive summary of fifty years of Swedish electoral research, where the case of Sweden is presented in a broad comparative framework, Holmberg and Oscarsson (2004) present the most comprehensive comparative analysis of party-leader effects to date.[3] The following year, Curtice and Holmberg published a longitudinal six-country comparison based on a different dataset (Curtice and Holmberg 2005). A volume edited in 2003 by Anthony King presents six country chapters plus a comparative summary; however, half of the cases are either presidential or semi-presidential systems and thus of lesser interest here (King 2003). A paper by Schmitt and Ohr (2000) presents a systematic longitudinal analysis of Germany. A broad comparative study, albeit with a more limited time frame, is offered by Curtice (2003).

To the extent that party leader effects on electoral behaviour are viewed as a central expression of the personalisation of politics, the results contained within Table I.2 do not seem to support the personalisation thesis. The comprehensive comparative analysis, conducted by Holmberg and Oscarsson, indicates that the independent effect of party leaders on voter behaviour is a fairly marginal phenomenon. Most notably, the alleged increase of leader effects over time – a core notion in the personalisation thesis – is found to be 'a myth' (2004: 175). However, a certain support can be detected for the hypothesis about a more prominent role for party leaders in systems where party polarisation is low. Moreover, leaders

3   This study will be summarised in English in Kees Aarts, André Blais and Hermann Schmitt, eds., *Political Leaders and Democratic Elections*, Oxford: Oxford University Press (forthcoming in July 2009) along with ten other chapters on various aspects of leader effects.

Table 1.2: Studies of party leader effects. Summary of main contents

Author	Focus	Empirical base	Results	Comments
Schmitt and Ohr 2000	Party preference, party vote	German electoral surveys 1961–1998	– Leader effects influence party preferences even after control for party identity (p. 16) – Leaders for major parties more important than those of smaller parties (Ibid.) – '… effects of a short time nature…. everything but a monotonic increase..' (Ibid.)	
Bartle and Crewe 2003	Leader effects	a) Detailed study of 1997 British election b) Compilation of evidence to form a times series 1964–2001	a) '… perpetuates… skepticism… about the … difference that party leaders' personalities make…' (p. 94) b) Weak, mainly contradictory evidence	
Brettschneider and Gabriel 2003	Relative effects of candidate evaluations and party identity	Survey data on Germany, 1961–1998	– '…the influence of… leaders is strongly mediated… by… partisan affiliation…' (p. 153) – '… no real evidence that personalization is a useful way of describing… German electoral behavior' (Ibid.)	

(Contd.)

Table 1.2: Studies of party leader effects. Summary of main contents *(Contd.)*

Author	Focus	Empirical base	Results	Comments
Curtice 2003	Effects of leadership evaluations controlling for TV consumption	CSES data 1996–2002	– '… very little evidence to support the claim that parliamentary elections have become presidential contests' (p. 15) – 'only limited support… that leader evaluations are relatively more important when party identification is low and attention to television is high' (p. 16)	Important comparative contribution, although with a limited time–span
Johnston 2003	Leader effects controlling for party affiliation, socio–economic group, region	Canadian elections 1988, 1993 and 1998	– '… more important the closer the party was to forming the government' (p. 179) – 'Net effects… much smaller' (Ibid.)	
King 2003	Four hypotheses: – Voters have likes and dislikes of leaders – They form an overall evaluation of leaders and candidates – These have a bearing on how they vote – The decisions often have a bearing on the outcomes of whole elections (p. 210)	Six states (USA, UK, Fra, Ger, Can, Rus), 1961–2001	– Very little influence on election outcomes, no trend over time (p. 213) – '… personality factors determine election outcomes far less often than is usually, indeed almost universally, supposed' (p. 220)	A fairly 'soft' comparison

(Contd.)

Table 1.2: Studies of party leader effects. Summary of main contents (Contd.)

Author	Focus	Empirical base	Results	Comments
Holmberg and Oscarsson 2004	Three hypotheses: – Individual candidates and leaders play a greater role in majoritarian than proportional systems – The importance of party leaders has increased over time – These effects strongest where the level of inter-party conflict is low	Longitudinal survey data from nine Western democracies (N= 375 163); time periods between 8 and 48 years.	–Independent party leader effects not strong anywhere 'with the possible exception of the USA' (p. 174) – Clearly stronger effects in majoritarian systems – The alleged increase of leader effects over time 'is a myth' (p. 175) – The hypothesis about inter–party conflict supported, but the correlation is not strong (Ibid.)	The most substantiated study so far
Curtice and Holmberg 2005	– Are voters more likely to vote nowadays for the party leader they like best? (p. 238) – Have leadership evaluations come to mean more when other factors are controlled for? (Ibid.) – Have people's evaluations of the parties increasingly become influenced by their evaluations of the leaders? (pp. 248–9)	A survey database on six West European countries (UK, Ger, Neth, Den, Nor, Swe), 1956–2001	– '…no sign that this is any more true than it was two or three decades ago' (p. 242) – '… while evaluations of party leaders may matter a little … it cannot be said that they matter much… there is simply no consistent evidence… of any kind of secular change in the importance of leadership evaluations' (p. 246) – 'Nothing much seems to have changed… The impact of leaders is… as variable and unpredictable as are human personalities themselves' (p. 252)	Strongly supports findings by Holmberg and Oscarsson

mean more when majoritarian rather than proportional electoral systems are used. Based on a different set of empirical data, the second longitudinal comparative study (Curtice and Holmberg 2005) arrives at virtually identical conclusions.

The rest of the studies surveyed in Table I.2 generally support these conclusions. Schmitt and Ohr (2000: 16) point to the lack of a clear trend over time. The other analyses, whether single-country studies or comparative surveys, unanimously underline the limited role of party-leader effects when party identity and other important factors are controlled for. Overall, the conclusion must be that the personality of party leaders is not among the prime determinants of electoral outcomes in parliamentary democracies.

Other studies
The remaining studies scrutinised for this book vary a great deal in terms of empirical focus. One of them is not an empirical study at all: Ian McAllister's essay 'The Personalization of Politics' in the authoritative *Oxford Handbook of Political Behavior* is an overview of earlier research rather than an empirical analysis in its own right. The other studies in this group have varying empirical foci. Notably, systematic comparative elements are all but absent in these studies. Moreover, a fairly strong focus on evidence originating from media characterises this part of the literature.

Table I.3 conveys a somewhat puzzling impression. McAllister's general overview makes a fairly strong statement in favour of the personalisation thesis. However, this study is not based on systematic empirical evidence; in fact the author does not really consider evidence against the thesis, although he does mention empirical data of this kind (McAllister 2007: 573–4). As concerns the empirical research examined in Table I.3, the picture is anything but clear-cut. Some studies, In particular Rahat and Sheafer's analysis of Israel (2007), present clear evidence in favour of the thesis. The authors find a stronger focus over time on individual politicians in three important respects; both institutional, media and behavioural personalisation has taken place. Similarly, Langer (2006) finds a growing focus on the prime minister in British news coverage. Three analyses of Germany represent the opposite extreme. From different angles, they present evidence that runs counter to the notion that politics in Germany is increasingly centred on individual politicians (Kaase 1994; Lessinger and Holtz-Bacha 2003; Schulz *et al* 2005). Two more studies on Germany are not as negative vis-à-vis the personalisation thesis (Lass 1995; Keil 2003); here, too, the evidence is somewhat mixed. The Finnish case seems to point in the direction of increased personalisation, but it is not particularly strong in terms of longitudinal data. Finally, the Belgian and Swedish studies contain data both in favour and against the personalisation thesis.

SUMMING UP: DIRECTIONS FOR FURTHER RESEARCH

One way of summarising the research so far is to look at the various country cases covered in the literature. In these cases, the conclusion must be that the question of the personalisation of politics is much less clear-cut than many authors (e.g. McAllister) seem to indicate. In fact, the issue is genuinely unsettled. There

Table 1.3: Other studies

Author	Focus	Empirical base	Results	Comments
Bennulf and Hedberg 1993	Media focus on individual politicians in coverage of party politics	– Eight Swedish newspapers four weeks prior to the elections of 1985, 1988 and 1991 – Attention to party leaders in three newspapers ten days before elections, 1956–1991	– The eight newspapers reveal no personalisation over time, in fact *less* personalisation regarding photographic content – The three-paper study points to a clear increase in focus on party leaders	–Evidence against personalisation based on a short time-span – The more clearly longitudinal study supports the personalisation thesis
Kaase 1994	– To what extent do mass media report on leaders? – 'Cognitive representation of political leaders in citizens' minds, and the leaders impact on voting decisions' (p. 213)	– Media in 1990 German election – Survey respondents who mention 'politicians' as 'strengths or weaknesses of parties' 1969–90 – Candidate images at three elections – Independent candidate effects on the vote, 1961–87	– Limited individual media exposure – Partisanship overshadows chancellor preferences – 'No evidence that candidate factors are growing in importance' (p. 226)	–Media data cross-sectional – What is the dynamic relationship between party leader evaluation and partisanship?

(Contd.)

Table 1.3: Other studies *(Contd.)*

Author	Focus	Empirical base	Results	Comments
Lass 1995	– Do voters increasingly refer to personal candidate traits when explaining their chancellor preferences and party vote?	Responses to open–ended questions in German electoral surveys in 1969, 1976 and 1986	– Personal traits mentioned more often, but not at the expense of party – Non-political traits not mentioned more often; no 'trivialisation' of politics	
Pekonen 1995	– Voter emphasis on candidate vs party – Candidate images as perceived by voters – Tendency to name governments, issues etc. after individual politicians	Tampere 1958 survey compared to national survey in Finland 1991	– Personalisation 'seems to be growing in Finland' (p. 206) – Clear increase 1958–91 in emphasis on candidates	Weak longitudinal data
Keil 2003	– To what extent do party campaigns focus on leaders and individual candidates? – Is there an increase in negative campaigning?	Electoral manifestos and advertising in national newspapers in Germany 1957–1998	– Personalisation has fluctuated over time; basic trend points to an increase – No clear increase in negative campaigning	

(Contd.)

Table 1.3: Other studies (Contd.)

Author	Focus	Empirical base	Results	Comments
Lessinger and Holtz–Bacha 2003	Role of candidates in parties' electoral advertising	Electoral advertising on German television, 1957–1998	– Formats without candidates dominate throughout – '…personalization in party spots is neither new nor increasing' (p. 2)	N not given
Van Aalst and van Mierlo 2003	Is there a growing focus on individual politicians in the media?	Two Flemish newspapers, 1958–1999	– No definite personalisation: both person and party gain exposure – Politicians figure more in headings and pictures	Fairly narrow empirical base
Schulz, Zeh and Quiring 2005	– Effects of media exposure on chancellor candidate preferences – Non-partisan voters expected to be more dependent on candidate preferences – The effects of chancellor candidate preferences on voting decisions expected to increase over time	Pre-election surveys in Germany in 1994, 1998 and 2002	– Mediatisation hypothesis only partially confirmed – Non-partisan voters most candidate–oriented – '…no evidence for an increasing determination of electoral choice by candidate orientation… [results] speak clearly against a personalization trend' (p. 73)	Short time–span

(Contd.)

Table 1.3: Other studies (Contd.)

Author	Focus	Empirical base	Results	Comments
Langer 2006	– Is there a growing focus on the British Prime Minister and his/her personal qualities and private life in news coverage?	– *The Times*, 1945–1999	– An upward trend for the overall visibility of Prime Ministers – Only a moderate positive trend for leadership qualities – More attention to the personal and private	Fairly narrow empirical base
McAllister 2007	– Party leader effects, presidential candidate evaluations – (To a lesser degree) all candidates – 'Presidentialisation'	Secondary sources	– 'Political leaders important not just for voter conversion but mobilization as well' (p. 583) – '[N]ow hold their positions by virtue of a personalized mandate' (Ibid.). – 'Considerable policy autonomy' (Ibid.) – 'Personalization of politics… perhaps *the* central feature… in the twenty–first century' (p. 585)	Not based on systematic empirical evidence, conclusions ignore evidence against the personalisation thesis (pp. 573–74)

(Contd.)

Table 1.3: Other studies (Contd.)

Author	Focus	Empirical base	Results	Comments
Rahat and Sheafer 2007	– Institutional p.: Changes in the nature of candidate selection – Media p.: candidate vs. party, personal traits vs. political performance in news reporting – Behavioral p.: Initiation and adoption of private member bills in legislature	Israel 1949–2003: – Inclusiveness of candidate selection on a scale 0–13 – 16 election campaigns in two leading dailies – 15 Knesset terms, laws based on private member bills as percentage of all bills passed	– '…clear and almost ongoing democratization' of candidate selection methods (p. 73) – Clearly increased media focus on candidates (p. 74) – Accelerating increase of legislation originating from private member bills (pp. 74–5) – Institutional personalisation is the primary impetus ('politics comes first') (pp. 70, 75)	The most broadly conceptualised study thus far
Johansson 2008	– Does election coverage increasingly focus on leaders over time?	– Morning press, tabloid press and televisions news in Sweden, 1979–2006	– No growth pattern in attention to party leaders or the visualisation of them – Clear growth in the dramatisation of party leader coverage	

are cases, Israel in particular, where strong evidence points towards and increasing personalisation. Analyses of Finland, and possibly Belgium, seem to support the personalisation thesis, although research is far from exhaustive. In still more cases – Britain, Sweden, and possibly Canada – research is simply too contradictory to permit an overall conclusion. Finally, possibly the most researched case of Germany presents so much contrary evidence that it might almost be called a negative case.

As to the alleged 'presidentialisation' of parliamentary systems – the ever more prominent role of prime ministers and party leaders – research hitherto might be summarised in the following way. The general 'gut impressions' of expert authors seem to be more in favour of the presidentialisation thesis than the actual evidence presented in the various country studies. This statement is not meant as a criticism but it could be assumed that the authors who agreed to contribute to the Poguntke and Webb volume are somehow generally sympathetic to the thesis. Interpretative assessments by intimate country expertise are often highly valuable in situations where systematic empirical data are not available or are extremely hard to come by. All political science issues are simply not readily measurable. However, more systematic comparative evidence would be needed to substantiate the rather strong conclusion presented by Webb and Poguntke in the concluding chapter: '[O]verall we feel confident, in view of the evidence set out in this book, that it is reasonable to talk of the 'presidentialization' of contemporary democracy' (2005: 347).

The most extensively researched part of personalisation studies (relatively speaking) concerns leader effects on electoral behaviour. Here, any overall conclusion must be negative from the point of view of the personalisation thesis: leaders' personalities and citizens' assessments of political leaders have not become a prime determinant of voter choice or electoral outcomes. They do have a discernible effect on voter choice, but this effect is dwarfed by such 'usual suspects' as party identity and preferences, as well as by socio-economic factors. In particular, the comprehensive comparative analysis presented by Holmberg and Oscarsson cannot be overlooked by future research.

The aspect that is probably least researched so far concerns the crucial question of citizens' perceptions of politics: to what extent has a view of politics as primarily a rivalry between individual leaders and politicians replaced the notion of politics as a struggle between collectively-defined interests and values in the minds of citizens? For want of such evidence, analyses of citizen appraisals of leaders and parties easily attain a somewhat mechanical character.

There can hardly be a more natural starting point for a comparative study of personalisation than to look for possible effects of institutional variation among countries. Political institutions belong to the core of political inquiry, and it is the specific task of political science to investigate their causal background, functioning and effects. Moreover, the conclusion presented by Rahat and Sheafer, whose study on Israel is among the most broadly conceptualised analyses of personalisation, emphasises the role of institutional change as a chief impetus behind the process (2007: 70–5). As for the kinds of institutions that should be highlighted, the interesting distinction is not between presidential and parliamentary systems.

It is neither exciting nor controversial to suggest that presidential systems by their nature direct attention towards individual leaders to a larger extent than do parliamentary systems. By contrast, the study of the effects of various electoral systems would seem a highly promising research area. Electoral systems have a strong bearing on the conditions of political leadership, campaigns and individual political careers. Differences in the degree of personalisation between countries and changes over time may very well reflect differences and changes in electoral arrangements.

Most of the empirical evidence understandably deals with political leaders. Politics can, however, also be personalised below the level of political leadership, i.e. as concerns the role of candidates. Among other things, there are interesting differences between electoral systems in this regard. A more general focus on candidates in addition to political leaders is therefore also called for.

Another area where comparisons are sorely needed concerns the role of media. While almost all authors point to media as both a cause of personalisation and an arena where it can be observed, basically all empirical evidence stems from single-country studies rather than systematic comparative accounts. Linguistic as well as other practical problems may make comparisons cumbersome in this field, but nevertheless, the role of media is so central that comparative efforts are simply indispensable.

As was noted earlier, citizens' perceptions of politics should be made the object of systematic inquiry. Do people today, and more so than in the past, perceive of politics as a rivalry between individual leaders and politicians rather than between collective interests, ideas and values? This is admittedly not an easy question to investigate empirically. Nevertheless, electoral surveys in several countries have for quite some time asked questions about the importance of various factors for the respondents' political choices. The importance of party leaders and the quality of candidates have frequently been among these. Some surveys also include questions about the political importance of individual politicians in general terms. Longitudinal data of this kind might offer one avenue of systematic inquiry into this question.

PLAN OF THE BOOK

This introduction is followed by four empirical chapters and a conclusion. Each of the empirical analyses uses earlier research as a point of departure but presents extensive new primary evidence as well. The themes of these chapters are chosen so as to shed light on several of the areas where so far research has not been particularly extensive.

The first empirical chapter focuses on personalisation in institutional terms. It starts out by discussing why institutions are important from the point of view of personalisation. In what ways may institutions enhance personalisation? The chapter argues that executive power and electoral systems are of paramount importance in this regard. The core of this chapter consists of two empirical analyses.

The first one deals with possible changes in the position of the prime minister in parliamentary systems, the second with the candidate-centredness of electoral systems during recent decades.

The second chapter examines the role of individual candidates. Are considerations about individual candidates becoming more important at the expense of party loyalties? The visibility of individual candidates varies widely among different electoral systems, and the chapter therefore analyses candidate importance separately for the various systems.

The role of party leaders forms the focus of the third empirical chapter. This area is relatively well-researched, and the chapter will start by offering an account of previous research on party leader effects in elections. The bulk of the analysis is, however, focused on the perceptions of citizens and voters as concerns the role of party leaders. Do citizens today have more intense views on party leaders than in the past? Does the explanatory power of party leader evaluation for party choice grow over time when other relevant factors are controlled for? Are there indications that party leaders will mean more to voters in the future?

The focus of the fourth and final empirical analysis is on how politics is presented, i.e. how the personalisation of politics is reflected in the media. While the importance of television for personalisation is underlined, the systematic empirical account offered in this chapter focuses on how newspapers have portrayed political leaders and candidates over the years. Newspapers represent a forum that allow for systematic longitudinal analyses more readily than other mass media.

For each analysis, data from several cases are provided. For some of the aspects studied, a fairly large number of cases can be treated in a uniform way. On some other points the analysis must be limited to a smaller number of cases and a 'softer' form of comparison. Overall, however, the analyses should provide a comprehensive answer to the question whether a general process of personalisation has taken place in stable parliamentary democracies.

chapter one | institutions and personalisation

The proper study of politics is not man but institutions

John Plamenatz

Recent decades have witnessed the re-emergence of institutionally-oriented analysis as a central field in the study of politics. In the heyday of behaviouralism, the study of institutions was frequently criticised for being overly preoccupied with the formal side of politics and thus for neglecting the reality of political life. The advent of 'new institutionalism' from the 1980s onwards, and the wave of constitutional engineering in the wake of the third wave of democratisation, have once again directed attention to the critical role of institutions in political life, as well as in the study of politics.

There is no need in the present context to argue extensively for the general importance of institutionally oriented analysis in political science. A rich literature is available to anyone looking for an account of various forms of institutional analysis in political science (e.g. Rhodes *et al* 2006). Rather, it is more relevant to say a few words about why it is important to include institutions in a study of the personalisation of politics.

The argument may be based on central lines of thought in some of the main varieties of institutional analysis (cf. Rhodes *et al* xii–xvii). One important orientation is rational-choice institutionalism. Rational-choice institutionalists view institutions as a set of behavioural incentives. Their basic assumption is that social life consists of individual utility-maximization within existing constraints. One important set of constraints is represented by political institutions that condition the behaviour of individuals. Depending on institutional design, alternative strategies can be effective in politics. A certain set of institutional constraints may enhance collective actions, whereas another institutional set-up may encourage individual actors to go it alone. Institutional variation and institutional change may therefore explain why the personal element in politics appears with varying strengths in different contexts or at different times.

Historical institutionalists emphasise the role of institutions as continuities. It is an intrinsic quality of institutions that they tend to preserve an existing state of affairs. Actors in power lean heavily on institutional continuity to preserve and to reinforce their positions. Those seeking to gain power may wish to upset institutions and replace them with new structures that help them preserve their power once they have gained office.

Sociological institutionalists see institutions as part of the culturally-defined norms that determine the values and expectations of citizens. If institutions elevate the role of individual leaders and politicians at the expense of more anonymous collective actors, the citizens tend to view this as 'normal' and expect politics to function this way. Again, it is easy to see that the conditions for individual actors are strongly dependent on the institutional environment in which they act.

Views of what constitutes an institution vary widely. The narrowest definitions equate institutions with constitutionally or legally-defined authorities; the study of institutions thus becomes synonymous with the analysis of constitutional blueprint. This is precisely what the representatives of the behavioural revolution had in mind when they criticised the 'formalism' of the previously dominant institutionally-oriented study of politics. The opposite extreme is probably represented by constructivist analysis that views institutions broadly as 'codified systems of ideas and the practices they sustain' (Hay 2006: 58). The founding fathers of new institutionalism, James March and Johan Olsen, employ a definition that represents the middle ground:

> An institution is a relatively enduring collection of rules and organized practices, embedded in structures of meaning and resources that are relatively invariant in the face of turnover of individuals and relatively resilient to the idiosyncratic preferences and expectations of individuals and changing external circumstances.

> March and Olsen 2006: 3

Indeed it's all quite relative! The definition by March and Olsen candidly portrays the difficulties in establishing clear lines of demarcation between institutions and non-institutions. To define institutions as merely a set of formal rules would be too narrow; the life of institutions – 'organised practices' in March and Olsen's language – must somehow be included. In order to be institutionalised, rules and practices must have a certain longevity. On the other hand, definitions must allow for the possibility of institutional change in the face of a changing environment – thus the 'relative' component in March and Olsen's definition.

The presents study looks for evidence for and against the assumption that central political institutions in parliamentary democracies have increasingly enhanced the position of individual leaders, and politicians as individuals, over the last decades. While it is important to use a concrete, down-to-earth approach to institutions, it would be overly limiting to just look for change in formal rules and regulations. An element of the concrete life of institutions, of organised practices within the formal confines of rules and regulations, must also be included.

This chapter has a dual focus. On the one hand, it portrays institutions that condition the role of political *leaders*; on the other hand, its looks for institutional evolution which is relevant to the position of individual candidates. On the first point, prime ministers, that is central political leaders in parliamentary systems, are at the centre of attention. Have the institutional conditions surrounding the prime minister changed and developed over the years so as to emphasise the individual leadership of the prime minister and focus political attention increasingly on the individual? As to the second aspect, the main question is whether electoral systems in parliamentary democracies increasingly centre on individual candidates instead of parties.

PRIME MINISTERS IN PARLIAMENTARY DEMOCRACIES

In a way, parliamentary democracy is a paradoxical system. In theory, parliament is all-powerful. The majority of the elected representatives can at any time throw the incumbent government out of office by a vote of no-confidence. In reality, power largely rests with the very government that is supposed to be at the mercy of the elected representatives. Overwhelmingly, policy originates from inside the executive leadership rather than the legislative chamber. True, there are fairly significant variations in the extent to which parliamentarians can exercise influence over the policy process. But, by and large, power over central political decisions in parliamentary systems rests with those who make up the government.

This being the case, the role of the cabinet leader, the prime minister[4], becomes of major interest to the present study. If a general personalisation of politics has taken place, one would expect this to be reflected in the role of the prime minister in parliamentary systems. In the institutional setting of parliamentary democracy, the prime minister can be expected to have become gradually more prominent at the expense of the rest of the government as well as the parliament.

To determine whether this indeed is the case is no easy task. No readily available objective measure exists for assessing the relative power of prime ministers, both cross-nationally and over time. Constitutional provisions are clearly inadequate in this respect. While they may give a fair idea of the general differences between various parliamentary systems, they suffer from two decisive weaknesses. In several cases, constitutions are almost silent as concerns the role of the prime minister. The United Kingdom has no written constitution; the Australian constitution does not mention the prime minister's office at all (O'Malley 2007: 8); the Norwegian constitution of 1814 is completely outdated on this as well as many other important points (Olsen 2002: 104–8), and so on. Second, important changes in the organised practices of government may take place without corresponding alterations in the constitutional blueprints. As will be evident from the following, only in a few cases have clear changes in the position of the prime minister been accompanied by changes in the written constitution.

In this chapter, two sources of empirical evidence are used to examine whether the position of the prime minister in parliamentary democracy has been elevated during recent decades. Both of these sources rely on judgmental data rather than on objective hard evidence, that can be easily measured, (although quantitative measures are applied in one of them). The first source is Eoin O'Malley's dataset on prime-ministerial power based on an expert survey among political scientists (O'Malley 2007). The second is the Poguntke and Webb volume on the presidentialisation of politics; in this volume, one central task for the various country specialists is to trace important changes in the 'executive face' of democratic politics during recent decades. O'Malley's data cover all governments in twenty-two parliamentary democracies from roughly 1980 through the first years of the 2000s.

---

4   Throughout this study, this expression will be used as generic term despite the fact that the cabinet leader in some systems is called the premier, chancellor etc.

Twelve cases included in the Poguntke and Webb volume qualify as parliamentary democracies. With the exception of those countries that later became democracies, the temporal baseline for analysis is approximately 1960 (Poguntke and Webb 2005: 18).

Have prime ministers become more powerful?
The O'Malley survey comprised the following countries that qualified as parliamentary democracies: Australia, Austria, Belgium, Canada, Denmark, Finland, Germany, Greece, Iceland, Ireland, Israel, Italy, Japan, Luxembourg, Malta, the Netherlands, New Zealand, Norway, Portugal, Spain, Sweden and the UK. The survey was sent to 413 experts on these countries. A total of 249 completed responses formed the empirical basis of the study. The response rate was just over 60 per cent, which is to be considered satisfactory in this context. The highest response rates were for Greece and Israel, both 72 per cent, whereas Portugal came at the bottom with a rate of 41 per cent completed surveys (O'Malley 2005: 303).

The survey aimed at estimating the level of prime ministerial 'influence over the policy output of the government' and the prime ministers' ability to get their 'preferred policies enacted' (O'Malley 2007: 11). In a world of academic research where questionnaires frequently comprise twenty to forty pages of detailed queries, the O'Malley expert survey seems remarkably short. For countries where coalition government is the norm, the number of questions was nine; for countries where one-party governments are the rule, only seven questions were asked. The experts were asked to rate each prime minister during roughly a twenty-year period. The average number of governments during the period was 6.3, and cross-national variation was modest: four countries were represented by five cabinets, seven by six cabinets and the remaining eleven by seven cabinets. Each survey question was to be answered on a nine-point scale, where 1 represented very little influence/control and 9 a great deal of influence/control.

The items of the questionnaire concerned following questions:
- The prime minister's freedom to select members of his/her own party as cabinet members
- The prime minister's freedom to select members of other government parties as cabinet members
- The prime minister's freedom to move and remove his/her own party's ministers from the cabinet
- The prime minister's freedom to move and remove ministers from parties other than his/her own from cabinet
- The prime minister's freedom to call an election
- The prime minister's power to restrict cabinet agenda
- The prime minister's power to set the cabinet agenda
- Government control over the agenda of parliament
- The prime minister's ability to get his preferred policies accepted and enacted

The survey, by and large, covers the core of executive power in parliamentary systems. Some of the questions, for instance the one about the prime minister's freedom to call an election, concern aspects of prime-ministerial power that can hardly be altered without changing the constitution. The other extreme is represented by the question about the prime minister's ability to get his preferred policies accepted and enacted. Here, it is quite imaginable that the prime minister's personal standing and leadership style, as well as current political constellations, may weigh in heavily. Taken together, nevertheless, the questions should give a fair idea of how the prime-ministerial institution functions in the twenty-two countries included in the survey. Any clear changes in the overall ratings can therefore be taken as signals of relevant change in the position of prime ministers. This is all the more true as O'Malley found the reliability, validity and comparability of his data to be at a sufficiently high level (O'Malley 2007: 13–16).

O'Malley himself was interested in cross-national variation rather than change over time. In the present study, cross-national variation is of less interest; the general position of the prime minister can be assumed to be the result of institutional differences between states. While change over time is the focal point here, it is not irrelevant to have a look at cross-national variation. These figures show the general patterns among countries and may help the reader to judge the reliability of the evidence at hand. Table 1.1 summarises O'Malley's results for each of the countries included in the survey. The scores reported represent the mean of the means that each of the prime ministers in each country received on the survey items.

There seems to be a certain association between cabinet longevity and prime-ministerial influence, but it is neither strong nor linear. As to cross-country variation, the data confirm the previously well-known fact that prime-ministerial power tends to be stronger in countries with single-member plurality electoral systems and one-party majority governments. Fragmented party systems in countries with proportional electoral systems tend to be found at the lower end of the table.

In order to detect any trends over time in the relative influence of the prime minister, O'Malley's data were examined in the following way. The prime-ministerial influence score for the first cabinet included for each country was subtracted from the score received by the last cabinet included for the same country. This provides a rough measure of the direction of possible change. Moreover, these figures were completed with information about the point in time when prime-ministerial influence peaked. For this purpose, the cabinets for each country were classified as *early*, *mid-period* or *late*. If the difference between the scores for the last and the first cabinet was positive and prime-ministerial influence, as measured in the survey, peaked late, then this provides the clearest evidence for increased prime-ministerial power over time. If, by contrast, the difference was negative and prime-ministerial influence peaked early, clear contrary evidence is at hand. The other possible combinations of these figures represent intermediate positions tending either towards increase, no change or decrease in prime-ministerial power.

Table 1.1: Country averages for prime-ministerial influence

Country	Number of cabinets	First cabinet in office (date)	Last cabinet out of office (date)	PM score
Canada	5	Mar 80	Nov 00	8.24
Malta	6	Dec 81	N.A.	7.16
Greece	6	Jun 81	Mar 04	7.10
Australia	7	Dec 84	Nov 01	6.98
Spain	5	Oct 82	Mar 00	6.92
UK	6	May 79	Jun 01	6.80
Luxembourg	6	Jul 79	Dec 01	6.50
Germany	6	Nov 80	Oct 02	6.29
Israel	7	Sep 84	Feb 01	6.21
Portugal	6	Jun 83	Dec 01	6.20
New Zealand	7	Jul 84	Aug 02	6.15
Netherlands	5	Nov 82	Apr 02	6.09
Ireland	7	Dec 82	May 02	6.08
Belgium	6	Dec 81	N.A.	6.05
Sweden	7	Mar 86	Oct 02	6.01
Denmark	7	Jun 84	Nov 01	5.77
Finland	5	May 83	N.A.	5.76
Norway	7	Jun 83	Mar 00	5.72
Austria	7	May 83	Feb 00	5.42
Italy	7	Jul 89	Apr 00	4.98
Japan	7	Nov 87	Apr 00	4.61
Iceland	7	May 83	N.A.	3.75
Total	**139**	**May 79**	**Mar 04**	**6.13***

*Standard deviation .943
Source: O'Malley 2007: 17–24

No definite trend emerges from Table 1.2. A number of cases, eight altogether, match our expectations of a generally increased prime-ministerial influence. These *affirmative cases* display higher PM scores at the end than at the beginning of the period and prime-ministerial influence peaked late in them. They are Australia, Belgium, Denmark, Finland, Iceland, Luxembourg, New Zealand and Sweden. On the other hand, there are six *contrary cases* where the pattern is reversed: Canada, Greece, Malta, the Netherlands, Norway and Spain. Another eight cases represent various *intermediate positions*: Germany, and possibly also Ireland, Italy and the UK are cases where the basic trend is towards increased prime-ministerial influence rather than the opposite; for Austria, Japan and Portugal it is difficult to detect any trend at all. Finally, in the Israeli case it is more appropriate to speak of a negative than a positive or neutral trend.

Table 1.2:   Trends in prime-ministerial influence in twenty-two parliamentary democracies

Country	PM score for last cabinet	PM score for first cabinet	Change	PM score peaked
Australia	7.83	7.08	+0.75	Late
Austria	4.14	4.28	-0.14	Mid-period
Belgium	6.77	5.75	+1.02	Late
Canada	8.14	8.50	-0.36	Early
Denmark	6.30	5.22	+1.08	Late
Finland	6.75	5.92	+0.83	Late
Germany	6.35	5.17	+1.18	Mid-period
Greece	7.15	8.50	-1.35	Early
Iceland	7.50	4.00	+3.50	Late
Ireland	6.40	5.70	+0.70	Early
Israel	5.31	6.08	-0.77	Mid-period
Italy	4.12	3.71	+0.44	Mid-period
Japan	5.00	5.79	-0.79	Late
Luxembourg	7.50	5.00	+2.50	Late
Malta	6.33	9.00	-2.67	Early
Netherlands	6.00	6.67	-0.67	Early
New Zealand	8.07	5.64	+2.43	Late
Norway	4.58	6.75	-2.17	Early
Portugal	4.71	5.00	-0.29	Mid-period
Spain	6.58	7.83	-1.25	Early
Sweden	6.81	5.91	+0.90	Late
UK	7.70	6.82	+0.88	Early

Source: Calculated on the basis of O'Malley 2007: 19–24.

All in all, there is slightly more change towards a strengthened institutional influence for the prime minister than there is evidence against the assumption. The main result is, nevertheless, that no general pattern exists. Of course, caution must be exercised when interpreting these results. Despite the fact that O'Malley's survey represents the most comprehensive empirical effort to date, the time period and thus the number of cabinets covered for each country is still too limited for the purposes of this book. Too many factors connected to specific political constella-tions surrounding given governments or having to do with the leadership styles of

unique individuals may affect the time-series surveyed here. It is therefore necessary to complement this scrutiny with a look at another set of analyses.

The 'presidentialisation' of executive power

In the Poguntke and Webb volume on the presidentialisation of politics, the authors of the various country chapters were asked to follow a common analytical
framework. Three 'faces' of presidentialisation formed the core of this framework:
the executive face, the party face and the electoral face. This section examines the
country chapters as concerns the first face. Focus will be on 'power resources,
including formal powers, staff and funding' (Poguntke and Webb 2005: 8). It is
equally important, however, to pay attention to the fact that prime-ministerial influence 'may increasingly be connected to the capacity to set agendas and define
the alternatives at stake' (ibid.).

In their comparative summary of the country cases, Poguntke and Webb noted
a 'shift in intra-executive power to benefit the leader' in all cases except Israel.
Israel is a special case as the country introduced a major constitutional reform
– direct election of the prime minister – in 1992. The reform was consequently
abolished, effective as of the 2003 elections. Moreover, for Denmark and Portugal,
Poguntke and Webb note that the increase in prime-ministerial influence started
from a low level (Poguntke and Webb 2005: 338).

The twelve parliamentary democracies included in the volume were, in order
of presentation: the UK, Germany, Italy, Spain, Belgium and the Netherlands (in
one chapter), Denmark, Sweden, Canada, Finland, Portugal and Israel. Below,
the central content of each country study as concerns change in prime-ministerial
power will be presented in a concise form. This will be done in the same order as
the country chapters appear in the original volume.

The United Kingdom. The authors note a 'considerable development of the
institutional resources at the disposal of the prime minister' (Heffernan and Webb
2005: 31). A general growth of the prime minister's staff has taken place. For
one thing, the PM now has his 'own diplomatic staff at Number 10' at his disposal (p. 35). This enables him to bypass 'the advice of the Foreign Office' (ibid.).
Moreover, and 'perhaps most important, "it seems likely that the potential for
prime-ministerial power within the state's political executive has been enhanced
due to structural changes which have generated a large and more integrated "executive office" under his or her control since 1970' (p. 56).

Germany. To begin with, Poguntke notes the absence of change in the formal
powers of the German Chancellor. 'This is, however, the only constant. As soon as
we move beyond a narrow focus on formal-constitutional powers, there are very
substantial structural changes' (Poguntke 2005: 67). Today, and more so than in
the past, German chancellors 'make use of the powerful machinery in the chancellor's office to screen individual ministers and coordinate government politics'
(p.81). One important area where prime-ministerial power has increased and that
has helped to boost his position in general is European integration (ibid.).

Italy. Italian executive politics have witnessed a 'growing autonomy of the prime minister's office and the exercise of an increasingly monocratic form of rule' (Calise 2005: 89). The prime minister's growing power has had several in-gredients: the increased use of emergency bills, the expansion of delegated legisla-tion and the growing cabinet control over the legislative agenda (p. 92). Several reforms have boosted prime-ministerial power. A 1988 law of 'the reorganization of the premiership' was quite important in this regard; further reforms in 2002 had the same effect: 'the improvements in its decision-making and policy-steer-ing capacities are unprecedented' (p.93). 'From being scarcely even *primus inter pares*... the prime minister has now evolved into by far the most prominent politi-cal figure in the nation' (p. 96).

Spain. The 1978 post-Franco constitution adopted the German chancellorship model 'with the explicit objective of ensuring executive dominance over parlia-ment, and prime-ministerial dominance within the executive' (van Biesen and Hopkin 2005: 109). However, the authors find '...no clear evidence of a gradual presidentialization... the new Spanish democracy was presidentialized from the very beginning...', whereas 'the status and autonomy of prime ministers have fluctuated' (p. 124).

The Low Countries. Fiers and Krouwel find a recent increase in the author-ity of the Dutch and Belgian prime ministers. Most of it has occurred without constitutional change. The exception is a 1993 reform of the Belgian constitu-tion providing for a constructive vote of no-confidence (Fiers and Krouwel 2005: 129). 'Despite... limited control over cabinet composition, prime ministers in the Low Countries have become more predominant because of an important change concerning their route to power... parliamentary elections have now turned into popular elections to decide the prime minister' (p. 131). Prime ministers today enjoy 'increasing decision-making autonomy' (p. 132), 'professionalization and expansion of the prime ministerial office' (p. 135), as well as 'growing longevity in office' (p. 136).

Denmark. In Danish executive politics, Pedersen and Knudsen find a 'centrali-zation of the cabinet around the "core" ministers and especially the prime minis-ter' (Pedersen and Knudsen 2005: 161). They underline the importance of regular EU summits in this regard (p. 163). When it comes to long term trends since 1960, they 'see a more general strengthening of the prime minister' (p. 166). Still, there are clear limits to this growth: 'Most significantly, though, prime-ministerial power in Denmark is still kept in check by consensus politics' (p. 174).

Sweden. The chapter on Sweden has a fairly strong focus on the then prime minister Göran Persson, considered by many to be one of the most powerful prime ministers in Sweden for decades. Aylott's study on 'How Sweden got President Persson' places a strong emphasis on the country's EU membership; according to him, it has 'given the government greater licence to act than hitherto' (Aylott 2005: 180). 'The pivot – usually, the Social Democratic prime minister... has come to resemble a more presidential figure' (p. 183). 'Cabinet ministers increasingly owe their appointment solely to the prime minister's patronage' (pp. 192–193). Aylott's study was written at a time when a strong social democratic prime minister was heading a government that was one in a long series of social democratic one-party governments. It is not immediately clear how applicable his conclusions are to the four-party bourgeois coalition in office at the present time.

Canada. The Canadian case, as portrayed by Bakvis and Wolinetz, is ambiguous. On the one hand, the Canadian system very much puts the prime minister on the centre stage in the Canadian parliamentary scene. His personal leeway is larger than in most comparable systems (cf. Table 1.1) On the other hand, 'executive dominance in a parliamentary system is not a new phenomenon. It dates back to the Diefenbaker and Trudeau eras' (Bakvis and Wolinetz 2005: 218). The authors do note that 'the prominence of the prime minister... became even more pronounced from 1993 to 2003 with the fragmentation of the opposition into four parties' (p. 218). On the other hand, the subsequent merger of the Alliance and the Progressive Conservative party reduced this fragmentation. In sum, while it is beyond doubt that the level of prime-ministerial influence is very high indeed in Canada, it is less clear whether one can speak of a trend towards stronger executive dominance in the Canadian case.

Finland. Finland is one of the cases where the growth of prime-ministerial power is clearest. The country gradually abandoned its semi-presidential form of government in the course of the 1980s and 1990s. Previously, during the prolonged rule of President Urho Kekkonen (1956–81), the Finnish political system at times resembled presidential government. The new constitution of 2000 codified the changes, leaving the president with little more than ceremonial powers. All of this has enhanced the role of the prime minister: 'Finnish government remains strongly partified in many ways, but there is no doubt that the prime minister enjoys significantly greater powers than hitherto. The rising power of prime ministers within the executive is based on their new-found autonomy from presidents, their leadership in setting the daily agenda of government, their importance in settling disputes within government (a job previously often done by the president), and their role as the conductor of Finnish policy towards the EU' (Paloheimo 2005: 257).

Portugal. The institutional development in Portugal is in many ways similar to that in Finland, but the formal changes occurred about a decade earlier in the Portuguese case. The 1982 constitutional reform signified a transfer from semi-presidential to parliamentary rule. In Lobo's words, it was 'a triumph for the prime minister' (Lobo 2005: 276). Moreover, the constitutional change was followed by an 'overall increase in resources available to the Portuguese prime minister since the 1980s' (ibid.). Overall, with the passage of time the Portuguese system has witnessed a 'growing concentration of intra-executive power around the prime minister' (Lobo 2005: 283).

Israel. Perhaps not surprisingly given the turbulent international setting of Israeli politics, Israel is a special case among the countries surveyed in the Poguntke and Webb volume. Hazan (2005: 290) speaks of a considerable period of '*de facto* presidentialization' prior to the change in 1992. 'In 1981 a new law was passed that allowed the prime minister to dismiss a minister – a power that until then he was not *legally* able to wield' (p. 291). Then in 1992, a quite radical constitutional innovation was introduced: direct election of the prime minister. Similar to presidential and semi-presidential systems, the position of the executive leader was directly anchored in popular will as manifested in election results. On the other hand, the popularly elected prime minister could be removed by major-ity vote in the Knesset. The intended consequences of the reform – a stabilisation of executive politics thanks to a decreased party system fragmentation – failed to materialise, and the system was repealed prior to the 2003 elections. As a con-sequence, several of the developments brought about by the 1992 reform were reversed (p. 307). However, this change has not been unambiguous: '... power resources and autonomy of the prime minister within the executive has [sic] been augmented by the repeal of direct elections'. 'The conclusion from the Israeli case is that the various attributes of *de facto* presidentialization need not go hand in hand' (ibid.).

Taken together, the chapters on countries in Poguntke and Webb convey a rea-sonably clear picture of the development of executive power in parliamentary de-mocracies. In eight of the dozen cases, the position of the prime minister has been strengthened over time. In yet another two cases (Canada and Spain), a clear trend over time cannot be discerned; however, these are countries where prime ministers have been strong throughout the period under examination. Israel, finally, displays a somewhat turbulent roller-coaster pattern that makes definite conclusions diffi-cult. It would be inaccurate, however, to characterise Israel as a negative case from the point of view of the hypothesis about strengthened prime-ministerial power. All in all, pressures to reinforce the position of the Israeli executive leader vis-à-vis parliament and the cabinet as collective have clearly made themselves felt.

Prime ministers in parliamentary democracies: conclusions
The two sources of empirical evidence examined above do not paint identical pic-tures of the development of prime-ministerial influence in parliamentary democ-racies. O'Malley's data indicate a growth in the influence of the prime minister in roughly half of the twenty two countries examined. The other half consists of countries where the development over time either runs counter to expectations or at least does not support them. The chapters on countries in the Poguntke and Webb volume, by contrast, lend these expectations considerable support. While our scrutiny of the text did lead to a few minor adjustments in the editors' con-clusions, the chief impression was that the role of the prime ministers has indeed been strengthened in the institutional setting of parliamentary democracy. Table 1.3 presents a summary of the results obtained from O'Malley's data and from the re-analysis of Poguntke and Webb. Only those cases that were included in both studies are included.

Table 1.3:   The development of prime-ministerial power in twelve
parliamentary democracies according to two sources

Country	Reanalysis of Poguntke and Webb	O'Malley
UK	+	(+)
Germany	+	(+)
Italy	+	+
Spain	0	-
Belgium	+	+
Netherlands	+	-
Denmark	+	+
Sweden	+	+
Canada	0	-
Finland	+	+
Portugal	+	0
Israel	0	(-)

Legend: + increased prime-ministerial influence, 0 no change, – decreased influence.
Parentheses indicate that the change is not particularly pronounced.
Sources: Chapters on countries in Poguntke and Webb 2005; O'Malley 2007: 19–24.

Comparing only those cases that were included in both sources, the differences between the two analyses become smaller. In a majority of the cases, the overall conclusion is identical or at least points in the same general direction. The only apparent exception is the Netherlands, where contrary conclusions emerge from the two sources of empirical evidence. Still, from a methodological point of view the comparison is difficult for several reasons. O'Malley's data include a larger number of cases, and several of the cases not included in the Poguntke and Webb lie outside the core of continental Western Europe: Australia, New Zealand, Japan, Malta, Greece and Iceland. There are also differences in perspective and method-ology. The chapters in the Poguntke and Webb volume were written with view to an assumed presidentialisation of politics. While there is no reason to doubt the expertise of the authors, they can be presumed to have been sympathetic to the general theme of the volume. The O'Malley dataset was based on questions in a questionnaire and in that sense not as clearly connected to a proclaimed theme. Also, the degree of standardisation is much higher in the O'Malley data than in the evidence from the Poguntke and Webb volume.

Therefore, considerable caution is in order when formulating a final conclu-sion on the basis of these sources. It is probably fair to say the following: *consider-able expertise seems to believe that there has been a growth over time in the influ-ence of the prime minister in the institutional setting of parliamentary democracy. Systematic empirical evidence suggests that this has indeed occurred in a large number of countries, but it would be exaggerated to speak of a pervasive and linear development across the universe of parliamentary democracy.*

MORE CANDIDATE-CENTRED ELECTORAL SYSTEMS?

With few and rather exotic exceptions (Anckar and Anckar 2000), democratic elections normally involve a choice between political parties. The parties that gain representation are, however, represented by individuals of flesh and blood. In the electoral process, these individuals are termed candidates. The role of individual candidates varies widely across electoral systems. In some systems, politics and parties present themselves through individual candidates; candidates are the 'face' of parties. In some others, the individual candidate is almost invisible in electoral campaigns. In some systems, the voter has a choice both between parties and between individual candidates; in others he simply casts a ballot for the party of his choice. Depending on these and several other factors, the incentive to conduct individual campaigns varies greatly. In some systems party campaigns predominate, in others individual candidates seeking personal support are the driving force behind elections. The aim of this section is to determine if the candidate-centredness of electoral systems in parliamentary systems has increased during recent decades. Have electoral reforms helped candidates gain prominence at the expense of political parties?

The relative importance of candidates as compared to parties can be determined in different ways; candidate-centredness is not a one-dimensional phenomenon. The factors that increase candidate-centredness may be interrelated to varying degrees, but they need not automatically go hand in hand. The present study follows a modified version of an operational scheme originally proposed by Carey and Shugart (1995). Their central concern is with the factors that determine whether there is a strategic incentive for candidates to run individual campaigns: do 'legislative candidates depend on their own personal reputations, as opposed to the reputation of their parties, to gain election' (Shugart 2001: 182)?

In the modified form presented by Shugart in 2001, the operationalisation is based on three factors. The first has to do with *who controls the ballot*? Is access to the party ballot controlled by party leaders or is it more open? May voters disturb the list order determined by the party?

Second, *who can benefit from a vote* given by an individual citizen? Do voters cast list votes or nominal votes? The greater the influence of the voters in determining which of the candidates become elected, the stronger the incentive for the candidates to run active individual campaigns. In closed-list systems, individual electioneering can only indirectly enhance the chances for an individual candidate to be elected. The list order determined by the party before the election is much more decisive in this regard. In some other PR systems, list order and other comparable features play a role, but the preference votes cast by voters may have an impact on the final results. In still other systems, preference votes for candidates are the only factor determining the order in which the candidates of a given party are elected (Carey and Shugart 1995: 420–1; Karvonen 2004: 206–8). Whether votes for candidates pool at the level of parties or party fractions is also of importance in this regard. If the chance of election of candidates always depends on the total vote of the party, they are well-advised not to compete too fiercely against candidates of the same party. If a vote for a candidate only benefits that particular candidate, candidates face few restrictions in designing their individual campaigns (Carey and Shugart 1995: 4212; Cox 1997: 45–6, 117–20).

Third, the incentive to cultivate a personal vote is affected by the *size of the electoral district*. If voters cast party-based votes, the incentive declines with increasing district size. If the districts are small, candidates can attract votes to their parties and thereby enhance their own chances. If voters cast nominal (preference or person) votes, increasing district size emphasises the importance of 'establishing a unique personal reputation to stand out in a crowded field of copartisans' (Shugart 2001: 183).

Shugart constructs an index ranging from 1 to –1 where the latter value indicates the highest possible degree of candidate-centredness. The original operationalisation of the three components of Shugart's index of candidate-centredness is presented below (excerpted directly from Shugart 2001: 183[5]). The figures denote the raw values on the basis of which the index values were calculated.

BALLOT

2 ballot access through approval of party elite only, and voters may not disturb order of list;
1 ballot access through decentralized internal party procedures, and voters may not disturb list;
0 ballot access dominated by parties, but voters may disturb list;
–1 ballot access in general election requires first surviving a preliminary round of popular voting;
–2 ballot access nearly unrestricted.

VOTE

2 vote for list only;
1 vote list or nominal, but list votes predominate;
0 vote is nominal only, but vote may pool or transfer to other candidates;
–1 vote is nominal or list, but nominal votes predominate and pool to other candidates;
–2 vote is nominal only and nontransferable.

DISTRICT

1 *District* magnitude greater than one, with *Vote* > 0;
0 *District* magnitude of one;
–1 *District* magnitude greater than one, with *Vote* ≤ 0, provided that *Ballot* ≤ 0.

For the purposes of this study the Shugart index was recoded so that 0 corresponds to maximal party-centredness, 2 to maximal candidate-centredness. The following examples of electoral systems/countries should give an idea of how this index works. Maximal candidate-centredness (value 2) is represented by the Single Non-

---

5 Reproduced with the kind permission of Elsevier.

Transferable Vote (SNTV) used in Japan prior to the reform of the mid-1990s. This is a system with multimember districts where votes cannot be transferred to other candidates or pooled at the level of lists or parties. Systems where parties control ballot access but voters may cast either a nominal or list vote in multimember districts have the value of 1.71, provided that nominal votes are the only criterion to decide which candidates are elected from the lists. In these systems – Greece is one example – a relatively small group of committed voters may help their preferred candidate become elected. The Irish single transferable vote (STV) represents the next level of candidate-centredness with the value of 1.57. The Finnish quasi-list system, where all voters must choose a preferred candidate from party lists and where preference votes pool at the constituency level, receives the value 1.43. Single-member plurality systems with two rounds (France, the USA) are rated 1.29, whereas the British plurality system with party control receives the value 1.14. These can be viewed as primarily *candidate-centred systems*.

Among the *party-centred systems*, the purest type is the closed-list proportional system. In these systems, there is usually a degree of decentralisation in the nomination procedures, which is why the value 0.20 is appropriate; Norway and Spain are examples of this type. The values 0.60–0.80 indicate a degree of preference voting in list systems. Such systems are in use in for instance Belgium and Denmark.

Mixed-member systems present a problem for Shugart's classification, since they contain two elements with different electoral logics. After careful consideration (Shugart 2001, 186–187), he classifies the German MMP system (also in use in New Zealand as of the 1996 election) as slightly party-centred (0.90 on our scale). The MMM system that was first applied in the 1996 Japanese election is neither classified as party nor candidate-centred and receives the value 1.00.

Is there any trend in the development of electoral systems among parliamentary systems? Before answering that question it is perhaps appropriate to remind the reader of the scope of this book: it concerns the alleged personalisation of politics in stable parliamentary democracies. New democracies that have opted for parliamentary government in connection with the most recent waves of democratisation fall outside the scope of this study. Therefore, this survey will not be concerned with the choice of electoral system in these more recent democracies.

A survey of the best sources (Lundell 2005; Gallagher and Mitchell 2008; the Johnson and Wallack *Database on Electoral Systems and the Personal Vote*[6]) shows that electoral reform is not particularly common among established democracies. For parliamentary systems, we have registered only thirteen cases of electoral reform.[7] Table 1.4 lists these cases and comments on the effects of the reforms on the candidate-centredness of the systems.

---

6   http://dss.ucsd.edu/~jwjohnso/espv.html

7   Minor technical reforms such as incremental redistricting or adjustments in regional representation due to population changes are not included. The temporary abandonment in 1985 of preferential voting in Greece is also excluded from the analysis; preferential voting was reintroduced after the subsequent 1989 election (Trantas *et al* 2006: 383–4).

Table 1.4: Electoral reforms in parliamentary democracies during recent decades

Country	Year*	Change	Effect on candidate-centeredness
Austria	1992	Increased number of constituencies, increased weight for preference votes	From 0.6 to 0.8
Belgium 1	1994	Possibility of expressing multiple preference votes	From 0.6 to 0.7
Belgium 2	1999	Weight of list votes reduced by half	From 0.7 to 0.8
Denmark	2007	Fewer and larger constituencies, St. Lagüe formula replaced by d'Hondt	Effect uncertain as of yet
Israel 1	1992	Direct election of prime minister	No effect on index, but greater focus on one person
Israel 2	2001	Repeal of direct election of prime minister	No effect on index, but less focus on one individual
Italy 1	1993	From open-list system to MM corrective**	From 1.71 to 1.00
Italy 2	2005	From MM corrective to a unique list system	From 1.00 to 0.00
Japan	1994	From SNTV to MM superposition	From 2.00 to 1.00
Malta	1987	Guarantee that majority of first preferences gives majority in parliament	No effect on index, but increased importance of having candidates that attract first preferences
Netherlands	1998	Candidate receiving 25% of electoral quotient declared elected***	Limited increase in MPs elected by preference votes, no effect on index
New Zealand	1993	From SMD plurality to MM corrective	From 1.14 to 0.9
Sweden	1998	From closed to flexible lists	From 0.2 to 0.6

* Year enacted

** Although this Italian system belonged to the same general category as the German and New Zealand systems, it contained somewhat stronger incentives for individual candidate activity (D'Alimonte 2008: 256–7).

*** Provided that party list is entitled to a seat (Andeweg and Irwin 2005: 88).

Sources: Andeweg and Irwin 2005, Gallagher and Mitchell 2008, Lundell 2005, Shugart 2001, Rihoux *et al* 2001, the Johnson and Wallack *Database on Electoral Systems and the Personal Vote* (http://dss.ucsd.edu/~jwjohnso/espv.html)

Again, the empirical evidence is mixed. In the list systems of Austria and Belgium, a stronger element of preferential voting has been introduced. In the Belgian case, two minor reforms in this direction have, in fact, taken place. Preferential voting in Netherlands had practically no effect between the Second World War and 1998; during that long period, 'only three candidates were elected by preference votes who would not otherwise have been elected according to their placement on the list' (Andeweg and Irwin 2005: 89). The 1998 reform increased the preferential element in the Dutch system, but it is still 'clear that the increase in preference voting has only a very limited impact on the composition of Parliament' (ibid.). In Sweden, the closed-list system was replaced by a flexible-list system. Even after these reforms, however, these systems remain among the primarily party-centred electoral systems. To this group, the Maltese case might be added. The 1987 reform did not change the formal role of candidates in the Maltese Single Transferable Vote (STV) system. However, as winning the majority of first preferences became the decisive element in Maltese elections, strong incentives were created for the parties to present candidates with a wide personal appeal in order to win a maximal number of first-preference votes.

The remaining cases of reform are either less clear from the point of view of candidate-centredness, or they are outright contrary cases. It is difficult to judge whether the recent (2007) Danish reform may affect the relative position of candidates (Gallagher and Mitchell 2008: xvi–xvii). If such an effect should manifest itself, it could be expected to increase very slightly the candidate-centredness of the system – at the present stage, however, this remains speculative. The changes in Israel did not concern the position of individual candidates. Still, one might say that the introduction in 1992 of the direct election of the prime minister increased the level of personalisation in Israeli electoral politics, and that this was reversed by the decision to repeal the system in 2001. Japan transformed from the most candidate-centred order to a neutral electoral system. New Zealand's system changed in the same direction, although the degree of change was smaller, from a slightly candidate-centred order to a weakly party-centred system. Finally, Italy presents the most spectacular pattern of change. The system used before 1993 was clearly candidate-centred, but the first reform replaced it with a neutral system. The 2005 reform then created a system that defies most classifications. All seats in the Italian Chamber of deputies were to be allocated using party list proportional representation with the entire country as a single constituency for seat allocation purposes. *Preference votes cannot be cast.* The real peculiarity of this system has to do with the special 'bonus' it awards to the winning list: 'The party or the coalition of parties that won a plurality of the votes nationwide was guaranteed to receive at least 340 seats out of the 617 "domestic" seats, while the losers would share the other 277' (Gallagher and Mitchell 2008: xiv). Thus a strong incentive against party system fragmentation was introduced in Italy. From the point of view of the present study, however, the main conclusion is that the system contains no discernible incentive to run individual campaigns. In fact, the reform introduced a system with the highest imaginable degree of party-centredness.

Overall, the analysis of the development of electoral systems among parliamentary countries bears many resemblances to the analysis of prime-ministerial influence. While there are several cases where the development seems to match our expectations of increased candidate-centredness, there are clear contrary cases as well. If a body of evidence as limited in scope as the one at hand allows us to speak of a general tendency, a cautious conclusion might perhaps be formulated in the following way: *The electoral reforms of recent decades have entailed a development towards a compromise between party and candidate-centredness. Several party-centred systems have become somewhat more candidate-centred, while some candidate-centred systems have become more party-centred.* But it must indeed remain a cautious conclusion.

SUMMARY AND CONCLUSIONS

The evidence presented in this chapter largely confirms the impression conveyed by the presentation of earlier research in the introduction. There is evidence of a growing importance of individual political actors both at the top level of parliamentary politics and as concerns the development of electoral systems. Taken together, this evidence involves a fairly large group of countries. Still, it would be incorrect to speak of a general trend. Too many cases present evidence that runs counter to the personalisation thesis; in some other cases it is difficult to pinpoint a clear trend at all. The evidence weighs more in favour of the thesis as concerns the development of prime-ministerial influence than the direction of electoral reforms. In the latter case, the limited number of relevant cases presents a problem. The conclusion must be that the personalisation thesis cannot be refuted on the basis of institutional evidence; but it would be stretching the evidence too far to say that the thesis stands corroborated.

chapter two | have individual candidates become more prominent?

I would vote for a pig if my party put one up

a British voter in the 1950s

Chapter 1 surveyed electoral reforms in parliamentary democracies in order to establish whether electoral systems displayed a trend towards a stronger emphasis on the position of individual candidates. While several examples of increased candidate-centredness in electoral systems were found, the overall result was mixed at best.

The present chapter focuses on the *behavioural* dimension. The central question is whether individual candidates have gained prominence at the expense of political parties in parliamentary elections, irrespective of whether the electoral system has been reformed or not. Are the qualities of individual candidates more important to voters today than in the past? Do parties increasingly emphasise the role of individual candidates in the election process? Do voters use the opportunity to cast preferential (person) votes, where available, more actively than they used to? These are some of the questions that will be answered empirically in this chapter.

From the point of view of the personalisation thesis, the study of individual candidates is just as relevant as the focus on party leaders (Manin 1997: 219; Swanson and Mancini 1996b: 10). Still, much less attention has been paid to candidates than leaders. One of the reasons must surely be the fact that it is impossible to create a generic measure of the position of candidates, which is equally applicable to all parliamentary democracies. While it is easy to describe the role of individual candidates in different electoral systems, a strict comparison of change over time is, in practice, ruled out. Let us, for instance, consider the relationship between the voters and individual candidates. Several possible measures that might be used to portray trends over time readily suggest themselves. One might ask whether citizens vote for individual candidates more than in the past. Alas, this would limit the comparison to those few countries that have flexible list systems, i.e. where voters may cast an optional preference vote for a candidate of their choice but are not compelled to do so. Other systems either compel the voter to cast his ballot for a candidate (Single-Member plurality/majority systems, STV, SNTV, the Finnish open list system) or do not allow for candidate votes (closed-list systems). Another possible measure would be the weight that voters assign to candidates, as opposed to parties when making their voting choices. As it turns out, however, very few electoral surveys or comparable opinion polls contain such questions. This also applies to another potential indicator, candidate recall. Very few electoral surveys allow for anything akin to time series that would show whether voters today remember individual parliamentary candidates better than they did some decades ago.

This means that a fully fledged comparative analysis, where countries are examined in the light of commensurable indicators, cannot be accomplished. Instead, a number of cases will be analysed separately with the aid of indicators that vary from country to country. The choice of indicators is made on the basis of applicability as well as availability. Due to institutional differences between parliamentary democracies, the applicability of indicators describing the position of candidates varies from case to case. Moreover, remarkably few electoral surveys and opinion polls have included questions about candidates. Rather unsurprisingly, the rule seems to be that surveys in those countries, where institutional features make the role of candidates visible, contain items about candidates. As to comparative international surveys, they either do not contain questions about candidates, or they present only cross-sectional data. The latter is the case with the Comparative Study of Electoral Systems (CSES). The first round of surveys (1996–2000) had a question about candidate recall, but it was not repeated in the more recent CSES surveys. Not even official electoral statistics always contain the kind of data that one might expect, given the electoral system in a particular country[8].

From a methodological point of view, however, the present analysis is not a classic comparative study where variation among cases is explained with reference to a given set of potential independent variables. Instead, focus is on the alleged change over time toward a more prominent role for individual politicians. The inclusion of a sufficient number of cases serves to broaden the empirical basis on which this alleged trend is examined.

Nine countries are examined empirically in the following analysis. Three of them belong to the same category in terms of their electoral systems. Belgium, Denmark and Sweden have flexible list systems where the voter may cast an optional preference vote. They differ from each other as regards the history of their individual system. The Swedish system with flexible lists has been used for a decade and applied at only three elections, whereas the Belgian and Danish systems have considerably longer histories. As to Finland, Ireland and the Netherlands the electoral formulas vary. However, these countries share two important features: they have multi-member constituencies, and voters must vote for a given candidate (in the Irish case, ranked candidates if a voter chooses to vote for several candidates). Therefore, Dutch and Finnish voters must choose between the candidates of a given party and Irish voters have the possibility of doing so. Germany represents the category of mixed-member electoral formulas. Finally, some very sketchy data will be presented for United Kingdom and Norway. These two countries, of course, have vastly different electoral formulas. They do, however, share one feature that is important in the present context. Voters in Britain and Norway cannot choose between several candidates for the same party. The nine countries will be presented in the order in which they have been mentioned here. In each case, a short description of the electoral system will be followed by a discussion about the indicators used, after which the empirical analysis itself will follow.

---

8   An example of this is Austria. The electoral system allows for an optional preference vote, but 'no official aggregate data are available on the use of preference votes' (Müller 2008: 408-409).

FLEXIBLE-LIST SYSTEMS

Belgium
The Belgian electoral system and the position of individual candidates within it have a long history. Only minor amendments have been added to the electoral formula that was introduced along with proportional representation in 1899. The system is applied to both chambers of the bicameral Belgian parliament, the House as well as the Senate. Candidates are presented on party lists in an order of preference determined by the parties internally. If a voter accepts the list order of the party of his choice he can endorse it by simply casting a list vote. Voters may, however, choose to cast a preference vote for a given candidate. To be elected, candidates must reach the electoral quota (the party's total vote in the constituency divided by the number of seats it receives, plus 1). Those candidates whose preference votes exceed the electoral quota are declared elected. If all seats that a party has won cannot be filled this way, list votes are added to the preference votes until all seats have been allocated. These list votes are distributed among the candidates according to their position on the list. Therefore, the list header almost always gets elected irrespective of his or her personal vote. If all list votes have been used before all seats have been assigned, the remaining seats are given to candidates with the highest preference votes (De Winter 2008: 421).

In practice, the Belgian variant of preferential voting has remained rather a weak one. Preference votes rarely disturb the list order determined by parties. This is illustrated by the oft-cited (De Winter 2008: 421; Rihoux *et al* 2001: 256; SOU 1993:21: 33) fact that less than 1 per cent of the MPs have been elected at variance with list order under this system since World War I. Two mechanisms explain this rather modest result of preferential voting. The first mechanism has already been mentioned: the list order determined by the parties strongly favours top-placed candidates. However, it is equally important that candidates highest up on the party lists normally receive a large number of preference votes as well. Many voters who choose to cast a preference vote do so in harmony with the rank-ordering presented by the parties. Such preference votes are of course no less 'genuine' than the ones that run counter to list order.

The electoral reform of 2000 contains the potential to allow more numerous MPs to be elected at variance with list order, as the number of list votes that can be used to top up the preference votes of the best-placed candidates was reduced by half. So far, however, the change produced by this reform in the actual composition of the Belgian parliament is marginal at best. Voters still seem to favour candidates at the top of the party lists when casting preference ballots (De Winter 2008: 422).

Longitudinal survey data that would show how Belgian voters view the importance of candidates to their voting choice and to politics in general have not been available. By contrast, an impressive time series depicting the use of preferential voting in Belgium can be used to portray change over time. These data go back to 1919. Between the world wars, the percentage of voters casting a preference vote was normally less than twenty-five. Table 2.1 presents decennial averages for preference votes since the 1950s plus the percentage of voters casting a preference ballot at the 2003 election. Separate figures are shown for elections to the two chambers of the Belgian parliament.

Table 2.1: Percentage of voters casting a preference ballot in Belgian parliamentary elections. Decennial averages 1950s–1990s plus percentages for 2003

Chamber	1950s	1960s	1970s	1980s	1990s	2003
House	23	37	48	48	55	67
Senate	22	30	38	36	53	68

Source: Calculated on the basis of Wauters 2003: 403.

In the 1950s, preference voting remained on roughly the same level as during the interwar years. After this point, the percentage of Belgians that utilise this option has shown a steady and fairly rapid increase. Up until the 1980s, preference voting was more popular in the House elections. From the 1990s, preference voting also rapidly gained popularity in Senate elections; today, it is in fact slightly more popular in connection with Senate elections.

The growing popularity of preference voting has affected the strategic behaviour of candidates, individual representatives as well as parties. In this dynamic process, it is sometimes difficult to distinguish between cause and effect. Individual representatives are today quite aware of the need to cultivate their ties with voters in their constituency. Parties have responded to the growing popularity of preference voting by increasingly placing well-known regional leaders on their lists. In fact, however, many regionally prominent candidates claim their right to stick to their positions at the regional level, thus giving up their federal seats for the benefit of other candidates. Similarly, MPs chosen as cabinet ministers give up their seats as Belgian ministers cannot be parliament members at the same time. All of this gives the parties a chance to retain control over the selection of MPs while at the same time capitalising on the personal vote. Still, as increasing numbers of candidates with a strong individual appeal occur on the party lists, the propensity of voters to cast preference ballots becomes higher and the parties must keep adjusting to this dynamic development. Apparently, the personal element is not quite as unimportant as one might conclude if the share of MPs elected at variance with list order were the only criterion (De Winter 2008: 422; SOU 1993:21: 33–4).

Overall, the Belgian development supports the hypothesis that individual candidates loom larger in the electoral process than they did in the past. The parties are by no means defenceless in this process. Quite the contrary, they have found ways of utilising the preferential element while at the same time maintaining a firm grip on the process of the actual selection of representatives. Representatives that gain seats in the Belgian parliament 'against the will of their parties' will probably remain exceptions for many years to come. Still there is no denying that the position of individual candidates is today more prominent in Belgian politics than it was some decades ago. In that sense, the Belgian case is an affirmative one from the point of view of the personalisation thesis.

Denmark

Denmark has a complicated electoral system in which both the nomination of candidates and the assignment of seats to parties and candidates take place in several geographical tiers. For the purposes of parliamentary elections, the country is divided into three regions, ten multi-member constituencies and ninety-two nomination districts.[9] The transformation of votes into the 175 'Danish' seats in the *Folketing* – four additional seats are reserved for the autonomous regions of the Faeroes and Greenland – several rounds of calculations are necessary. Prior to voting, parties have to decide the format in which they wish to present their candidate lists to the electorate. These layers convey an impression of complexity in the Danish system that makes it all but impenetrable to the non-expert.

As demonstrated by Jørgen Elklit with commendable clarity (2008: 457–65), the system is not quite as inscrutable as the first impression may indicate. For the purposes of this study, many of the technical details of the Danish electoral process may in fact be omitted. What is important to note for the present purpose is that a) the electoral formula in Denmark is a highly proportional list system; b) voters may cast an optional preference vote but are not compelled to do so, and c) the parties can affect the significance of preference votes by choosing one of two forms of organising their candidate lists. The two latter points are of particular importance in the present context, as the relationship between parties and individual candidates depends on both the choice of the voters and the choice of the nomination format by the parties.

The role of candidates in the electoral process in Denmark has not been a central theme in Danish election research (Thomsen and Elklit 2007: 307). It is not possible to construct time series showing how Danish voters have viewed the importance of individual candidates in their electoral choices. The 2005 Danish Election Study did, however, focus on this aspect. It was found that no more than 9 per cent of the respondents mentioned local candidates as a reason for their voting choice (ibid.: 309). As no comparable data are available for earlier elections, there is no way of knowing whether this figure is high or low in a historical perspective.

There is, however, ample longitudinal evidence on both the way parties have utilised the alternative nomination formats and the extent to which voters have cast preference votes. These two indicators will be used here to detect possible changes in the position of individual candidates in the electoral process.

The two main types of electoral lists that the parties can present are what Elklit (2008: 463) terms 'standing by (nomination) district' (*kredsvis opstilling*) and 'standing in parallel' (*sideordnet opstilling*). Here they will, for the sake of sim-

---

9   The 2006 electoral reform redrew the borders of the three regions and reduced the number of
     constituencies and nomination districts. Still, the basic structure of the electoral system remained
     unaltered.

plicity, be called 'party-oriented lists' and 'open lists', respectively. In both cases, the voter can choose between a list (party) vote and a preference vote. It is in the distribution of these votes that the two list formats differ from each other. Under the party-oriented option, the party indicates its preferred candidate by placing him or her at the top of the candidate list and printing his/her name in bold type. This candidate will be credited his/her preference votes plus the party list votes in his/her nomination district. There are, on average, nine nomination districts per constituency, and it is at the constituency level that the lion's share of seats are allocated.[10] Therefore, top-placed candidates in large nomination districts have a clear advantage over candidates in small districts, because the larger districts will carry more numerous list votes. There is also a variant of this list format where parties rank all candidates; this type amounts to a practically closed party list.

Under the open-list option, all candidates are entitled to a share of all list votes in each nomination district. In each nomination district, candidates receive a portion of the list votes corresponding to their personal vote in that district. At the constituency level, list votes and preference votes from each nomination district are aggregated to make up each candidate's total votes. Casting a list vote therefore means that the voter leaves it up to other party supporters to decide which of the candidates should be elected. This list format often helps locally popular candidates to gain major portions of both the preference and list votes. At the same time, it contains an incentive for constituency-wide campaigning as there are both preference and list votes to be won throughout the constituency.

In Table 2.2 the incidence of open lists at Danish parliamentary elections since the 1960s is shown with averages for the percentage of voters casting preference votes since the 1950s.

Table 2.2: Percentage of open lists and preference votes in Denmark since the 1950s/1960s. Decennial averages

	1950s	1960s	1970s	1980s	1990s	2000s
Open lists as per cent of all lists	N.A.	13	44	52	76	88
Percentage of voters casting a preference vote	52	42	47	47	50	49

Sources: (a) Open lists: SOU 1993:21, 37; www.djh.dk/samf/1semF04/PS1105-OH.pdf.;
    Elklit 2008: 466–7; www.indenrigsministeriet.dk
    (b) Preference votes: Statistical yearbook, Danmarks statistik, various years

If the expectation was that candidates have become more important at the expense of the parties in Danish elections, the empirical evidence in Table 2.2 conveys a paradoxical message. On the one hand, there has been rather a

---

10   135 of the 175 seats; the remaining 40 are national compensatory seats.

spectacular growth in the use of open lists on the part of the Danish parties. Today, open lists are the rule, after having represented a small minority of all lists in the 1960s. Only parties on the extreme left wing – and not even they in all constituencies – opt for party-oriented lists. Parties have accepted it as a predominant norm that the choice of the individual candidates should be left up to the voters. In this sense, preferential voting has become clearly more important when it comes to the personal composition of the *Folketing*. Yet it seems as if the voters have not really noticed this change. The level of preferential voting has remained basically the same during the last half century. The most noticeable change was the *decrease* in the percentage of preference votes in the 1960s. Since that time, roughly half of those voting have cast preference votes. Preference votes mean more, but still half of the electorate clearly indicates that it is only the party composition of the Danish parliament that matters to them.

From the point of view of the personalisation thesis, Denmark stands out as both an affirmative and a contrary case. By opting for open lists, parties clearly indicate that they view the role of individual candidates as increasingly important in the electoral process. At the same time, the voters show no signs of assigning increased importance to candidates.

Sweden

Until 1997, Swedish electoral law prescribed a closed-list system. Parties presented a slate of candidates, and voters cast list votes only. In 1997, an electoral reform allowing for optional preference voting was passed by the Swedish parliament. The system was first applied in connection with the 1998 parliamentary election.[11]

The fact that preferential voting is optional means that voters can continue to cast party votes only if they so wish. Party votes are distributed to the candidates according to the list order determined by the parties. If voters use the preference vote option, they must mark one of the candidates on the party list with an X. For a candidate to be elected at variance with list order, he or she must have received a minimum of 8 per cent of the party's total vote in the constituency. If the number of candidates whose preference votes qualify them for election is smaller than the total number of seats won by a party in a constituency, the rest of the seats will be filled according to list order. In many ways, this form of preferential voting introduced in Sweden resembles the Belgian preference vote (Holmberg and Möller 1999: 7).

The political significance of preferential voting has been rather limited. Party popularity and the list order determined by parties continue to be the decisive factors behind the selection of individual MPs. Most preference votes were given to candidates who would also have been elected if list order had been the only criterion. In 1998, twelve out of the 349 members of the *Riksdag* were elected at variance with list order. In 2002 this figure was thirteen, in 2006 no more than six. The percentage of such MPs thus declined from 3.4 to 1.7 in eight years (Oscarsson and Holmberg 2008: 273).

---

11 It had, however, been tried out in seven municipalities already in connection with the 1994 election.

Sweden has a national Election Studies Programme that dates back to 1956. In terms of coverage in time and space, it is probably the most comprehensive election studies programme in the world. The present book may therefore profit from the work done within this programme. Still, given the general scope of Swedish election research, it is safe to say that individual candidates have not been a major focus over the years. In many ways, electoral surveys in Sweden prove the rule that election research largely reflects the way the electoral system works. Before 1998, questions concerning individual candidates were scant in the Swedish surveys. Since the 1997 reform such questions have started to appear in the electoral surveys.

There is, however, one survey question that has been asked ever since 1956, although it was dropped from the surveys in 1973–82 (four parliamentary elections). This question measures candidate recall; respondents were simply asked to name a candidate from their constituency in the most recent parliamentary election. Table 2.3 shows the development over time in the periods 1956–70 and 1985–2006.

Table 2.3: Candidate recall in Sweden in 1956–1970 and 1985–2006. Percentage of voters who could name a candidate from their constituency in a post-election survey

1956	1960	1964	1968	1970	1985	1991	1994	1998	2002	2006
60	55	56	60	49	48	44	45	44	40	41

Source: Oscarsson and Holmberg 2008: 279
Legend: Includes only those respondents who had voted in the respective elections.

The development in Sweden is intriguing, and it is not good news from the point of view of the personalisation thesis. Candidate recall has dropped roughly twenty percentage points in the last half century, and the introduction in 1998 of preferential voting had no effect whatsoever on this seemingly unstoppable development. The continued decrease since 1998 in the percentage of those voters who remembered the name of a candidate is all the more striking as the electoral reform meant that at least a portion of the electorate consciously indicated a given candidate as their favourite. In fact, the 2006 election survey revealed that only 58 per cent of those who had cast a preference ballot remembered which candidate they had voted for (Oscarsson and Holmberg 2008: 279).

For the period since 1998 there are official election statistics (see www.val.se) concerning the use of the preference vote. They repeat the pattern evident in the latter half of Table 2.3. In 1998, 30 per cent of those voting opted for a preference vote. Four years later this figure had declined to 26 per cent and at the 2006 election no more than 22 per cent of the voters cast a preference ballot. When the electoral reform was being planned, it was estimated that 'between 30 and 50 per cent of the voters will vote for particular candidates to a Riksdag election' (SOU 1993:21, 204). Subsequent elections have shown that this estimate was clearly too high.

At the same time, voters have not become increasingly critical of preferential voting as a constitutional feature. In fact, the share of respondents who welcome the possibility of casting a preference vote has increased slightly, as is evident from Table 2.4.

Table 2.4: Swedish voter opinions about preferential voting 1998–2006. Percentages

	1998	2002	2006
There should be no preferential voting	17	17	14
There should be an element of preferential voting, but it should be smaller than in this year's election	12	13	12
There should be an element of preferential voting, and its magnitude was right in this year's election	44	46	54
The element of preferential voting should be increased in future elections	14	13	12
No opinion	13	11	8
Total	**100**	**100**	**100**

Source: Oscarsson and Holmberg 2008: 274.
Legend: The question asked was formulated as follows: 'Generally speaking, what is your opinion about preferential voting in Swedish parliamentary elections? You can choose one of the following alternative responses'.

Taken together, the Swedish data point to the following conclusion. Individual candidates have not become more important to the voters over the years. In fact, they seem to have become less prominent in the minds of the electorate. Voters recall individual candidates less frequently than in the past and the introduction of preferential voting has not reversed or stopped this development. The use of the preference option has declined, although a clear majority of the voters are sympathetic to the idea that the option itself should be available. Freedom of choice in this regard is welcomed but the clear majority of Swedes indicate that it is the parties, and only the parties, that matter to them as far as parliamentary elections are concerned. Sweden is, if anything, a negative case from the point of view of the personalisation thesis.

SYSTEMS WITH COMPULSORY PREFERENCE VOTING

Finland

The Finnish list system with compulsory preferential voting was established in 1955. It was in fact a by-product of an electoral reform, the main purpose of which was to simplify the electoral system and to restrict the practice of a candidate running in several constituencies simultaneously. While this latter ambition was not fulfilled, a system of preferential list voting was created that has been in use ever since. It is doubtful whether the majority of the legislators actually realised that it was a new preferential list system on which they had decided (Törnudd 1968: 57).

The act of voting is simple and straightforward in Finland. The ballot paper contains an empty circle where the voter is supposed to write in the number of his candidate of choice. The candidates with their individual candidate numbers appear on the party lists; the normal practice is that the parties list their candidates alphabetically. The seat allocation to the 200-hundred seat unicameral parliament[12] takes place entirely at the constituency level. Using the D'Hondt method, the number of seats for each party list or electoral alliance in each constituency is first calculated on the basis of the total number of votes that the lists have received. After that, the seats are filled with candidates according to the number of preference votes that they have received. Popular candidates for major parties often help candidates with a fairly modest number of personal votes become elected; while at the same time even quite popular candidates representing minor parties frequently fail to gain a seat due to the limited vote totals of their lists.[13]

Finnish electoral research has not been particularly comprehensive, and electoral surveys have been few and far between. It is only in the 2000s that anything like a permanent Election Studies Programme has appeared in Finland.[14] However, as voting for individual candidates is a compulsory feature of the Finnish electoral system, earlier electoral research has always paid some attention to how voters view the role of the candidates. The standard question has been whether candidate or party weighed more heavily when voters cast their ballots. This question was asked in the very first post-election survey conducted in Finland. Voters in the 1958 parliamentary election in two Finnish municipalities were asked about their behaviour. One of the municipalities was Tampere, an industrial city; the other Korpilahti, a rural community. These two communities represented widely-differing political environments. Tampere had a left-wing majority, thanks to the prominence of industrial workers, but also a strong conservative following. In Korpilahti, by contrast, the Agrarian Union was by far the strongest political party. Of the Tampere respondents (N=388), 80 per cent said that party was more important to their voting choice, 15 per cent that it was the candidate; 5 per cent could not say. For the Korpilahti sample (N=75), the corresponding figures were 73, 17 and 10 per cent (Pesonen et al 1993: 73). Thus it seems that irrespective of local party structure, voters overwhelmingly stressed the importance of party over candidate in the 1950s. Although not comparable with national surveys, these figures provide an interesting early point of reference for more recent survey results.

---

12 *Eduskunta* in Finnish, *Riksdagen* in Swedish.

13 In fact, an electoral reform is currently being planned to modify this feature of the system. The immediate backdrop of this plan is the failure of the Green Party leader and cabinet minister Tarja Cronberg to gain a seat in parliament.

14 See www.uta.fi/laitokset/politiikka/henkilokunta/Paloheimo_research_plan_2007-10.pdf

National post-election surveys have asked the same question in connection with the 1983, 1991, 2003 and 2007 parliamentary elections. Table 2.5 presents the results of these surveys.

Table 2.5: The relative importance of party vs candidate to Finnish voters 1983–2007. Percentages

	1983	1991	2003	2007
Party	52	51	49	48
Candidate	42	43	47	51
Cannot say	6	6	4	1
Total	**100**	**100**	**100**	**100**
(n)	(993)	(1141)	(1004)	(1172)

Sources: Pesonen *et al.* 1993: 72–4 (1983and 1991), FSD1260 (2003), FSD2269 (2007)
Legend: The question was formulated as follows: 'In the final analysis, which was more important to you, party or candidate?'

During the past quarter century, the propensity of voters to stress candidate over party has increased. The change has not been fast or dramatic, but the trend has been reasonably clear. In the 2007 post-election survey, those stressing candidates were for the first time both more numerous than those who named party and exceeded 50 per cent. The change is due to a decline in both the share of those who stress party and the percentage of those who cannot say.

Interestingly enough, when two surveys in the 1990s (1995 and 1999) asked the same question about the *next* election – that was almost four years away in both cases – the importance of candidates was even more pronounced. In 1993, 50 per cent of the respondents said candidate would mean more in the next election, 37 per cent named party; 13 per cent could not say. In 1999, the corresponding figures were 56 per cent for candidate, 34 per cent for party and 10 per cent for cannot say (Paloheimo 2005b: 213). Of course, speculating about one's motives at an election that lies several years ahead is different from explaining one's vote in an election that was recently conducted. Still, these figures too indicate that the propensity of respondents to emphasise the importance of candidates has increased over time.

Overall, it seems warranted to speak of a stronger voter emphasis over time on candidates as opposed to parties. Still, it is important to stress that the way respondents answer this survey question does not constitute hard evidence on causality. On the basis of these data we know how respondents 'feel like answering' rather than what really determines their voting behaviour (Bengtsson and Grönlund 2005:231). It is hardly likely that voters first survey the candidate lists of all parties and then decide about their voting choice. Most voters probably limit the range of acceptable party lists to one or two. But if increasing numbers of voters choose to stress person over party when answering a survey question, this at least tells us something about the social acceptability of a more personalised approach to politics. In this sense, the figures presented here bear witness of increasing personalisation.

Political parties have long been aware of the advantages of running candidates with a broad personal appeal on their lists. For at least half a century, concerns have been voiced that Finnish politics is becoming 'Americanised' as a consequence of various 'celebrities' running on party lists. It has not been rare that candidate lists have included persons known to the general public primarily from the world of entertainment or sports. However, the occurrence of such persons in parliament itself has largely been a marginal phenomenon of very little importance (Petersson et al. 1999: 138). Critics of the Finnish electoral system and elections in Finland should focus on not that 'celebrities become politicians', but rather the eagerness of politicians to become celebrities. Due to the importance of personal candidate appeal in elections, incumbent MPs are often keen to gain publicity by appearing on television shows and in other contexts, which have limited direct relevance to politics (Karvonen 2002: 36).

A growing concern about individual campaign finance also manifests in Finland. Many candidates spend considerable amounts on their individual campaigns (Ruostetsaari and Mattila 2002: 97–101). As of 2000, all elected MPs must account for their campaign finance to the Ministry of Justice (Gidlund 2004: 108). This legislation indicates that the role of individual candidates has also become more prominent from a financial point of view.

Taken together, data on Finland support the notion that individual candidates have gained prominence in the electoral arena. While the change is not rapid or dramatic, there seems to be a fairly steady growth in the weight and salience of individual candidates in electoral politics in Finland.

Ireland

The Single Transferable Vote (STV) system used in Ireland since 1922 is in some ways a paradoxical phenomenon. On the one hand, the act of voting is easy and citizens do not seem to have any trouble fulfilling the requirements of a valid ballot. On the other hand, the calculation of the final election results is a complex process that still sometimes takes several days to complete (Farrell 1997: 123). Students of voting systems have long been fascinated by STV, and the system would probably be one of the most popular contenders if experts on electoral systems were asked to name their favourite. Apart from Ireland, STV is the primary system for parliamentary elections only in Malta. The Australian senate is also elected by using STV, while the rest of the empirical examples concern regional or local elections in parts of the English-speaking world.

When explaining the limited spread of STV, cultural and linguistic factors can clearly not be overlooked. However, the position of political parties in STV systems must also be considered. Unlike other proportional systems, STV makes party control of citizens' electoral behaviour quite difficult. As it is normally parliaments dominated by political parties that are the key actor in constitutional reform processes, it is fairly natural that electoral reforms have resulted in formulas other than the Single Transferable Vote (Farrell and McAllister 2003: 17).

STV is a clearly proportional electoral system (Lijphart 1986: 175–6), yet it lacks a central element found in other PR systems in use: the party list. In STV systems, candidates are fielded in multi-member constituencies; as in other PR systems, the proportionality of the election outcome is related to constituency size. In Irish Dáil elections, all candidates in a constituency appear in alphabetical order on the same ballot paper. Today, the information provided about each candidate includes name, party, party logo, place of residence and occupation. Until 1963, no information about party affiliation was printed on the ballot paper. In order to cast a valid vote, voters must mark one or several of the candidates on the ballot. If they choose to mark several candidates, they must write 1 beside the candidate of their first choice, 2 beside their second choice, and so on.

By using the Droop quota (Farrell 1997: 116), the minimum number of votes necessary for election is first calculated. Those candidates, whose first-preference votes entitle them to a seat, are declared elected. If there are still seats to be filled in the constituency, the surplus votes of the elected candidates are then distributed, according to the distribution of the second preferences on those ballots that had the already elected candidates as first preference. Should there still be vacant seats after this round of calculations, the candidate with the lowest number of first preferences will be eliminated from the race and his or her votes transferred to the other candidates (Gallagher 2008: 514–520; Gallagher and Mitchell 2008: 593–6).

As indicated in Chapter 1, STV is one of the most candidate-centred electoral systems in existence. As party control of the ballot is limited, one might expect that a highly fragmented party system would result. However, the level of party system fragmentation in Ireland has been relatively low compared to the family of list PR systems. Two features in particular have contributed to this. On the one hand, a persistent feature of Irish politics has been the cleavage between more radical and moderate nationalism, pitting Fianna Fáil against basically all other parties. Most importantly, limited constituency size (four seats on average) has given Fianna Fáil and its chief rival, Fine Gael, a large-party bonus that has countered the tendency towards fragmentation. An indication of this tendency is instead to be found in the relatively high number of independents in the *Dáil* (Gallagher 2008: 520–3).

STV provides the voter with a broad range of alternatives. He can vote for his favourite candidate only; he can vote for a straight party ticket by giving preference to the candidates of one party only; he can add candidates of other parties after giving his highest preferences to candidates of his favourite party; or he can mix candidates irrespective of party affiliation. Under such a system, the strategic goals of a party – to maximise the party's share of the vote and minimise that of rival parties – and the goals of individual candidates – to maximise their own chances of election – are frequently at odds. Unlike proportional list systems, candidates have no way of directly profiting by large vote totals for their party under STV. In fact, candidates of a party are each other's rivals as much as they are rivals of other parties' candidates. Therefore, they frequently need to appeal to voters beyond regular party supporters in their constituencies. Personal campaigns and local constituency work are essential to candidate success (Marsh 2003: 117–18).

The qualities of STV make Ireland a particularly interesting case from the point of view of the personalisation thesis. It is all the more regrettable that there is so little in the way of longitudinal data on Irish electoral behaviour. The first nation-wide election study was conducted in connection with the general election of 2002, a fact that makes longitudinal analyses in the Irish case difficult. Sparse survey data must be patched together from various sources, which, of course, limits comparability to a considerable extent.

A potentially interesting question concerns ticket-splitting versus party loyalty. Party loyalty can be operationalised as 'the proportion of the transferred votes that stays within the party when the votes from one of the party's candidates have been transferred and at least one other candidate of the same party is available to receive transfers' (Sinnott 1995: 209). While it may, at first, seem that transfers within a party are a sign of party loyalty and split-ticket voting an indication of an orientation towards individual candidates, the issue is not quite as simple as that (see also section on Germany below). The question of party size strongly affects the propensity for ticket-splitting. If a voter's favourite party is a minor one, chances are that it will only field one candidate in the constituency. Casting a party ballot would then mean abstaining from the chance to give several preference votes and thereby increase the chances that one's vote might make a difference. Richard Sinnott, who has studied party loyalty in the light of election statistics in Ireland between 1948 and 1992, has noted that the general success of parties at an election also makes a difference:

> ...party loyalty can decline significantly either when the party does very badly and when it does extremely well. This is presumably because, on the one hand, a fall in a party's popularity can be reflected not just in a fall in its first preference vote but a fall also in the loyalty of and reliability of transfers from those who do decide to give it a first preference vote. On the other hand, party loyalty may be reduced when the party's vote shows exceptional increases because the party attracts voters who have not previously voted for it and may not vote for the full party ticket.

> Sinnott, 1995: 209

Sinnott examined the way preference votes were transferred within and between parties at general elections from 1948 to 1992; included were the three main parties: Fianna Fáil, Fine Gael and Labour. The above-mentioned effects of general party success and party size were clearly visible in his data. The patterns for Fianna Fáil and Fine Gael tended to fluctuate roughly the same way over time. In both cases, party loyalty decreased in the course of the 1980s and reached an all-time-low in 1992. For Fianna Fáil, the drop between 1989 and 1992 was from 77 to 69 per cent; for Fine Gael the corresponding figures were 72 to 64 per cent, respectively. For Labour, the pattern of fluctuation is much stronger. The general conclusion for Labour must nevertheless be that 'Labour loyalty is substantially less than of the two other main parties' (ibid.: 211). All in all, these figures give some support to the expectation of decreasing party loyalty over time; the changes are nevertheless far from conspicuous and the trend by no means linear (ibid.: 209–11).

Sinnott also examines a phenomenon termed *plumping*. It 'occurs when a vote for a party becomes non-transferable in a situation in which all of the candidates of the party in question have been elected or eliminated, but in which the vote could transfer to other parties and candidates and thus... affect the destination of a further seat or seats' (ibid.: 211). Plumping can be seen as an 'extreme' or even 'perverse form of loyalty. From the individual voter's point of view, and assuming the intention of maximising the effect of the vote on the outcome, plumping is irrational' (ibid.).

An analysis of the three main parties reveals that high levels (up to 80 per cent) of plumping characterised Fianna Fáil until the late 1970s. From this date onwards the basic trend was downwards, and at the 1992 election an all-time low of little over 40 per cent was reached. As for Fine Gael, plumping increased until 1981, being over 60 per cent. From there on, the pattern of decline was very sharp. At the 1992 election, plumping was down to a little over 10 per cent. Again, the pattern for Labour reveals generally lower levels than for the two main parties. Here, too, a sharp decrease between 1989 and 1992 can be noted. All in all, these data too bear witness of decreasing party loyalty over time.

These figures can be supplemented with data from the 2002 national election survey as to what extent votes cast sequential party ballots. This expression refers to those voters that limited their preferences to candidates of one party only. According to the survey responses, 48 per cent of voters who had a Fianna Fáil candidate as their first preference voted for such a 'straight party ticket'. For Fine Gael the figure was 40 per cent and for Labour 36 per cent (Marsh 2007: 507). Although not directly comparable with Sinnott's data, these figures indicate that party-centred voting has continued to decrease.

Occasional surveys in Ireland have asked respondents whether party or candidate mattered more to their vote choice. Figures are available for 1979, 1989 and 2002. The response alternatives were not identical in these surveys, but they do provide a basis for some conclusions. Table 2.6 shows how responses have evolved over time.

In 1979, a majority of the respondents considered party to be more important than candidate. By 1989 this gap was down to merely two percentage points even if respondents were also given the alternative that party and candidate were equally important.[15] When in 2002 respondents had to choose either party or candidate, the latter alternative was clearly more frequently chosen. The importance of candidates was accentuated by the second question asked in 2002. Even when respondents could choose the alternative 'depends on party' it was clear that the importance of candidates was greater than that of parties: 46 per cent would have voted for the same candidate regardless of the candidate's party affiliation. In sum,

---

15 Seven per cent of the responses were not accounted for by Sinnott.

even given the degree of incommensurability between the three surveys it seems that respondents are increasingly prone to stress candidate over party when explaining their voting choices.

Table 2.6:   The importance of party vs candidate in Ireland in 1979, 1989 and 2002. Percentages

1979	Which was more important to you, the candidate himself or herself, or was it the party they were standing for?		
	Party	Candidate	Don't know
	51	46	4
1989	Which was more important to you, the candidate himself or herself, or was it the party they were standing for?		
	Party	Candidate	Both equally
	40	38	15
2002	Which would you say was more important in deciding how you cast your first-preference vote – the party or the candidate him/herself?		
	Party	Candidate	N.A.
	41	59	N.A.
2002	If this candidate had been running for any of the other parties would you still have given a first-preference vote to him/her?		
	No	Yes	Depends on party
	38	46	16

Sources: For 1979, Irish Opinion Poll Archive; for 1989, Sinnott 1995: 171; for 2002, Marsh 2007: 511, 523.

Ireland is a highly interesting case when it comes to studying the relative importance of parties and candidates to the electorate. In the future when the national election surveys have produced more longitudinal data, Ireland will provide ample opportunities for detailed studies in this field. Despite the scarcity of data today, however, it seems warranted to conclude that the Irish case supports the notion of the increasing importance of individual candidates as compared to parties.

The Netherlands

The Dutch electoral formula has remained basically the same since 1917, when majoritarian elections were replaced by proportional representation. Although the extension of suffrage to women in 1919 and the abolition of compulsory voting in 1970 represented important changes in the electoral process, they did not affect the way in which the electoral system works. Under the Dutch system, voters must cast a ballot for an individual candidate; the option of a pure party list vote does not exist. Still, the formula is not a strongly candidate-centred one, as list order determined by the parties plays a powerful role in deciding which candidates actually get elected (Andeweg 2008: 492–3).

The system is an extremely proportional one, as the 150 members of the Dutch lower house (*Tweede Kamer*) are in practice elected with the entire country as a single constituency. The country is divided into 19 electoral districts, but as parties have a possibility of pooling their district lists, the districts have mainly an administrative function. All parties that field candidates in more than one district utilise the option of combining their lists at the national level. Parties are then allocated seats according to their shares of the vote at the national level (ibid.: 493–6).

Concerning individual candidates, parties normally place their party leaders on top of the candidate lists, followed by the other candidates in the preference order determined by the parties internally. Total list votes decide the number of seats that a particular party wins. The candidates are elected according to list order. However, candidates whose preference votes amount to at least 25 per cent of the Hare quota necessary for winning a seat will be assigned seats irrespective of list position (Andeweg and Irwin 2005: 88).

Traditionally, preference votes have not had much of an effect on the composition of the Dutch parliament. List position has been the overshadowing factor, and most candidates who have received sufficient preference votes to be elected with the aid of them would have been elected thanks to their list positions as well. The 1998 reform specifying 25 per cent of the Hare quota as threshold has nevertheless given preferential voting greater potential.

Voters who simply want to support a certain party give their preference vote to the first candidate on the party's list. This person is called the 'list-puller' (*lijst-trekker*). Preference votes (*voorkeurstemmen*) in Dutch parlance refer to votes for candidates other than the list-puller (Andeweg 2008: 494). From the end of World War II until 1998, only three MPs were elected at variance with list order. At the 1998 elections, two candidates managed to do this, as did one candidate per election in 2002, 2003 and 2006 (Andeweg and Irwin 2005, 88; www.vrouwenbelaagen.nl/politiek/verkiezingen). The usual way to measure the share of preferential voting as compared to party voting is to calculate the share of votes for candidates other than the list-pullers. Table 2.7 contains decennial averages for preferential voting since the Second World War.

Table 2.7:   Percentage of Dutch voters casting a preference ballot, 1946–2006. Decennial averages

1940s	1950s	1960s	1970s	1980s*	1990s	2000s
3	5	10	10	12	20	20

Legend: Votes for candidates other than the one at the top of the list
* Includes elections in 1981, 1982 and 1986; figure for 1989 missing
Sources: 1946–1986: www.politiekcompendium.nl and Hessing 1985; 1990s: estimate by Andeweg and Irwin 2005: 88; 2002 and 2003: Andeweg and Irwin 2005: 88; 2006: http://vrouwenbelaagen.nl/politiek/verkiezingen

Only a tiny minority of the Dutch voters used the option of voting for some other candidate than the 'list-puller' during the first two postwar decades. The proportion of voters using this option gradually increased during the 1960s, and since the 1990s around one-fifth of those voting use this option. The active use of preference votes for female candidates has been an important part of this increase (Hessing 1985: 168; http://vrouwenbelaagen.nl/politiek/verkiezingen). Preferential voting is still an exception rather than the rule, and MPs who are elected at variance with list order continue to be a fairly marginal phenomenon in Dutch politics. However, the overall trend seems to point to an increasing attention to individual candidates over time.

TICKET-SPLITTING IN A MIXED-MEMBER SYSTEM: GERMANY

In a succinct formulation, Eckhard Jesse characterises the German electoral system as 'a system of proportional representation, restricted by a 5 per cent clause, with a personalized element' (quoted in Saalfeld 2008: 212). Although the details of the system have undergone several changes, notably due to German reunification, its most important features have been stable since the electoral reforms of the 1950s. Since 1956, the following elements have been central to the system. Half of the now 598 'regular' members of the *Bundestag* are elected from single-member constituencies, the other half from closed party lists at the level of the *Länder*. Voters cast two ballots: one for a constituency candidate, another for a party list. Only parties that win at least 5 per cent of the vote nationally or a minimum of three constituency seats participate in the proportional distribution of seats. As parties are allowed to pool their list vote at the national level for the determination of their share of the seats, the proportional distribution of seats corresponds to the parties' relative popularity at that level (not counting those parties who fail to pass the 5 per cent hurdle). Those parties that win more single-member seats than their national list vote percentage would indicate are granted surplus seats (*Überhangmandate*) in the *Bundestag*.

The legal threshold for election has clearly dampened the effects of proportionality on the German party system. The effective number of parties with parliamentary representation has normally been under three in the postwar era. The surplus seats have also contributed to a fairly concentrated party system, as normally only the largest parties have a chance of gaining local constituency seats (Saalfeld 2008: 211–19).

The German electoral system is quite special when it comes to the relationship between voters and individual candidates. The politically decisive part of the election takes place in a closed-list system where voters have no way of promoting a particular candidate. At the same time, they are expected to pick a local constituency candidate in a single-member district. Although this part of the election does not permit an intra-party candidate choice in the same way as the systems described above, this part of the German system was designed with the intention of creating a strong 'personalised' bond between the local electorate and the local representative (Klingemann and Wessels 2001: 279). The important question in the present context is if the system has worked as intended and whether the trend is toward a stronger personalised element in German electoral politics.

The importance of individual rank and file candidates has not received a great deal of attention in electoral surveys in Germany. Attention is instead directed to those party leaders who stand out as potential candidates for chancellorship (ibid.). Longitudinal survey data are therefore not available to investigate how voters have viewed the role of ordinary *Bundestag* candidates for their voting choices. However, Klingemann and Wessels (2001: 296) argue that ticket-splitting can be seen as an indication of 'a personal vote at the grass roots'. Therefore, trends in ticket-splitting can be regarded as at least indirect evidence of the importance assigned by voters to individual candidates.

It would, of course, be overly simplistic to conclude that every time a voter casts a ballot for different parties at the SMD and party list levels, he or she does this in the former case because of the candidate's personal qualities. In fact, in the debate on ticket-splitting among German political scientists it has been held that ticket-splitting is to be regarded wholly or overwhelmingly as an example of strategic voting. Voters, especially supporters of smaller parties, want to maximise the chances for a certain party coalition in government. As SMD seats are difficult to win for small parties (Jesse 1988: 112), these voters vote for the 'lesser evil' of the large parties at the SMD level. If this is the case, the qualities of the SMD candidates need have little bearing on the decision to split the vote (Saalfeld 2008: 220–1). However, with the aid of a detailed analysis of German election results, Klingemann and Wessels reach the conclusion that strategic voting is an important but not predominant element in ticket-splitting: '...on average, the proportion of strategic voters... remains at the level of about 40% of all ticket-splitters' (2001: 287; cf. also Gschwend 2007: 19).

In Table 2.8 the decennial averages for ticket-splitting in German *Bundestag* elections is presented for the past forty five years.

Table 2.8: Ticket-splitting in Germany 1961–2005. Decennial averages for the percentage of voters who voted for different parties in the two electoral tiers

1960s	1970s	1980s	1990s	2000s
6	7	12	17	24

Sources: For 1961–1998, Klingemann and Wessels 2001: 288; for 2002, Gschwend and van der Kolk 2006: 164; for 2005, Forschungsgruppe Wahlen 2005: 113.

Split-ticket voting in Germany has quadrupled in the course of the past five decades. Strategic coalition voting is an important component of ticket-splitting, but its relative share of all ticket-splitting has probably not increased. According to the analysis by Klingemann and Wessels of the period 1976–1998, strategic coalition voting peaked in the 1980s being a little over half of all ticket splitting. From this time, its relative importance declined. 'We can safely conclude from these findings that one can identify a sizable group of citizens whose voting patterns indicate that the nominal and list votes are used to express different party or candidate preferences' (Klingemann and Wessels 2001: 288). This conclusion was supported by an analysis of cross-sectional data on SMD candidates as compared to party list candidates as well as a large survey in 1998 on voters at the constituency level. SMD candidates emphasised their ability to win votes and the importance of constituency work to a significantly higher degree than party list candidates. As for voters, their perceptions of candidates' constituency work significantly affected their voting choices in local constituencies (ibid.: 289–95).

Ticket-splitting does not merely reflect the voters' wish to influence the composition of government coalitions. It is also an expression of a will to influence the choice of individual legislators. As there has been a marked increase in split-ticket voting in Germany over the past five decades, the conclusion must be that the German case lends support to the expectation about increased candidate importance.

SYSTEMS WITHOUT CANDIDATE CHOICE: BRITAIN AND NORWAY

The seven parliamentary democracies examined above provide the voter with an opportunity to make a choice among individual candidates while at the same time not forcing him to give up voting for his favourite party. The scope of this choice varies from the broad range of alternatives provided by the Irish STV system via the preferential list systems of several Western European countries to the possibility of ticket-splitting in Germany between the SMD constituency vote and the politically decisive party list vote. Limiting the analysis to these systems would, however, result in a one-sided picture of parliamentary democracies. Many parliamentary systems do not give the voter an opportunity to choose simultaneously between parties as well as candidates. Closed-list systems, quite common among parliamentary democracies (Karvonen 2004: 208), present the voter with a slate of rank-ordered candidates that the voters have to take or leave. Single-member plurality systems do the same in the singular: choosing a party means having to accept its sole candidate in the constituency. In this section, Norway represents the former system, the UK the latter. In both cases the central features of the electoral system have been stable basically throughout the democratic period (Narud and Valen 2007: 55–63; Mitchell 2008: 158–61). In Norway, a prolonged parliamentary debate in the 2000s about a transition to a system with preferential voting has not resulted in any reforms. A 2001 survey among voters also disclosed that the majority of Norwegians were against preferential voting (Narud and Valen 2007: 64–7)

Unfortunately from the point of view of the present analysis, the position of individual candidates in countries without candidate choice has not attracted much attention on the part of electoral researchers. Questions dealing with the relative importance of candidates as opposed to parties are normally not included in electoral surveys in these countries. As no preferential voting exists, official statistics do not contain anything either that might be used to measure the varying importance of candidates. In a word, there is an acute shortage of adequate evidence of the kind that would be needed here.

This section will have to content itself with some rather sketchy and unsystematic data on candidate recall in Great Britain and Norway. The idea is that heightened candidate importance should manifest itself as higher levels of candidate recall over time. Even this question has to be portrayed with data from several, and not identical, sources. Since the items in the various surveys were not formulated identically, comparisons over time as well as across cases must be treated with some caution.

A few early election surveys in Britain asked the respondents whether they remembered the name of the candidate that was elected for their respective constituency. Norwegian election surveys had comparable, but not identical questions in 1969 and 1985. Both countries were included in the first wave of CSES surveys (1996–2000) where a question on candidate recall was included. Table 2.9 shows the results of these surveys. All years included are election years, and data originate from post-election surveys.

Table 2.9:   Candidate recall in the UK and Norway, various years

Country	Year	Question	Per cent correct answers
UK	1966	Do you happen to remember the name of the candidate who was elected to parliament for this constituency?	81
	1970	Do you happen to remember the name of the candidate who was elected to parliament for this constituency?	83
	1997	Do you happen to remember the name of any candidates who stood in your constituency in the last parliamentary election?	60
Norway	1969	Can you name any of the candidates on the list that you voted for?	64
	1985	Can you name one or several of the candidates on the various party lists in your county in the parliamentary election of this autumn?	67
	1997	Do you happen to remember the name of any candidates who stood in your constituency in the last parliamentary election?	68

Sources: UK 1966 and 1970, courtesy of Professor Richard Topf, Centre for Comparative European Survey Data (CCSESD); Norway 1969 and 1985, courtesy of Professor Bernt Aardal, Norwegian Election Studies Programme; both countries 1997, CSES data cited in Holmberg and Oscarsson 2004: 187.

More than four out of five British voters in 1966 and 1970 were able to name the local MP correctly. The difference compared to the 1997 survey may at least partially be a result of the way the questions were formulated. It is possible that some respondents interpreted the 1997 question to mean 'candidates besides the incumbent MP'. This is, however, speculative. What one should be able to conclude from the figures is that candidate recall has at least not improved in Britain. As for Norway, the stability of the figures, despite varying formulations of the questions, is rather striking. The Norwegian figures are so stable that they cannot be used as evidence in favour of the personalisation thesis. Overall, these admittedly meagre data from two systems without candidate choice do not indicate that the role of individual parliamentary candidates has become more pronounced over the years.

SUMMARY AND CONCLUSIONS

The realities of empirical research frequently compel scholars to resort to comparisons between apples and oranges; this chapter is no exception. Systematic evidence based on identical indicators across cases is simply not available. Still, the second-best solutions that form the core of the empirical analysis in this chapter make it possible to summarise the findings in a comparative fashion. This is done in Table 2.10.

Table 2.10: Candidate salience in nine parliamentary democracies. Summary of findings

Country	Indicator	Candidate salience: trend
Belgium	Share of voters who cast a preference vote	+
Denmark	Share of parties that present open lists	+
	Share of voters who cast a preference vote	0
Sweden	Candidate recall	−
	Share of voters who cast a preference vote	−
	Voter acceptance of preferential voting as option	+
Finland	Share of respondents who stress candidate over party	+
Ireland	Ticket-splitting/plumping	+
	Share of respondents who stress candidate over party	+
Netherlands	Share of voters who cast a preference vote	+
Germany	Ticket-splitting	+
UK	Candidate recall	(0/−)
Norway	Candidate recall	0

Generalising from a population of merely nine cases is always risky; it is all the more difficult as the summary does not point to any indisputable trend. Clearly, there are cases where data point to an increased role for individual candidates. But there are also cases where no trend or even a negative development from the point of view of the personalisation thesis can be discerned. Still, the positive signs appear to outweigh the negative ones. In fact, stretching the empirical evidence to its limits, one might speak of the following trend in the data. *In those countries where the possibility of choosing between individual candidates has existed for a long time, the relative importance of individual candidates seems to have increased.* Denmark is a partial exception, as preferential voting has not become more popular, although parties today overwhelmingly opt for the open list format in their nominations. In Sweden, the decade-old preferential option was used less in the most recent elections than when it was introduced. Simultaneously, a slightly increasing number of Swedes, in fact a majority, feels that the option should be there. Be that as it may, preferential voting has not stopped the decline in candidate recall among Swedish voters. As to those systems where candidate choice is not available to party supporters, no growth in candidate recall can be discerned.

In sum, the expectation that individual candidates have become more prominent in parliamentary elections over the years does receive some support in the empirical analysis. The support is not strong or unequivocal, but it is there. Still, it is important to remember that in none of the cases is the position of individual candidates a particularly central issue in parliamentary politics. The decisive issue is, and will continue to be, the relative strength of the parties. However, that strength may in the future increasingly come to be affected by the fate and behaviour of individual parliamentary candidates.

chapter three | leaders and citizens

A central – perhaps the central – element of the personalisation thesis is that the role of party leaders has been strengthened at the expense of parties as collective bodies and ideological communities. Today, so the argument goes, citizens increasingly take their cues from party leaders as persons rather than from party platforms and collective party identities. It is on the basis of their evaluation of party leaders rather than policy platforms that citizens formulate their political preferences. When they cast their ballots, they increasingly vote for leaders instead of parties. All of this has profound implications for electoral politics:

> The trend towards the emphasis on leaders is likely to further exacerbate the decline in political parties, since their programmatic function is being steadily absorbed by the major party leaders who, in any event, hold a personalized rather than a party mandate. There may be greater electoral volatility, which is already occurring as a result of partisan dealignment and the declining political influence of social structure. As leaders come and go, and electoral mobilization and conversion comes increasingly to depend on political personality rather than party program, there is scope for even more electoral volatility. At the same time, election campaigns will become more important in determining outcomes, featuring personal images as much (or more than) parties and policies; this is already a trend which is one of the more visible consequences of personalization.
>
> McAllister 2007: 584

The focus of this chapter is on the relationship between party leaders and voters. Is it indeed the case that voter evaluations of leaders today loom larger in the electoral process than a few decades ago? Is this a linear development? Have there been temporal and geographical variations in the growth of the importance of leaders in parliamentary politics?

As we saw in the Introduction, a fair amount of evidence has already been presented in this particular area of personalisation research. Most of the studies surveyed in the Introduction dealt with party leaders in one way or the other. In relative terms, a particularly solid body of research has been presented as concerns the question of leader effects on electoral behaviour and party choice. Whatever

---

16 Quoted in King 2003, 2

contribution the present book wishes to make concerning the relationship between leaders and citizens it must take this previous research as a point of departure. Therefore, a short summary of the main studies of party leader effects in elections will be presented before formulating the specific queries addressed in this chapter.

PREVIOUS RESEARCH SAYS 'NO'

As noted in the Introduction, a survey of empirical studies of leader effects on voters makes rather disheartening reading from the point of view of the personalisation thesis. The predominant result is negative: independent leader effects in elections are limited and there is not much evidence to suggest that these limited effects have increased over time.

There is of course no need to repeat the overview of research that was presented in the Introduction. However, the three most important comparative contributions should be dealt with in somewhat greater detail than was possible in the general overview. To a higher degree than most other analyses, these studies can claim generalisable findings. They are both cross-national and longitudinal in structure. They are based on separate sets of empirical evidence, which is why they complement rather than repeat each other. Most importantly, they essentially support each other's main conclusions.

Holmberg and Oscarsson's study (2004) of party leader effects in elections in nine Western democracies is the best substantiated analysis to date. Primarily based on data from the *Leadership Project,* this analysis examines the relative importance of leader evaluations and party evaluations for party choice among nearly 400,000 respondents. For most of the cases included, data cover several decades. Results based on a series of regressions are straightforward. With the exception of the USA, party evaluations are a clearly stronger predictor of party choice than are party leader evaluations. For the USA, the result is hardly surprising as data originate from presidential elections and presidential candidates are equated with party leaders. Moreover, and most importantly, nothing indicates that the relative importance of leader evaluations is increasing over time. There are, to be sure, interesting differences between countries. Countries with majoritarian elections display stronger leader effects than countries where proportional electoral systems are used. Where ideological polarisation is low, leaders tend to mean more than where ideological competition is more intense.[17] Overall, however, party evaluations predominate over party leader evaluations, and nothing indicates that a change is under way (Holmberg and Oscarsson 2004: 174–5).

The 2005 study by Curtice and Holmberg examines similar questions with the aid of the *European Voter Database.* The database contains integrated election surveys for six Western European countries (Denmark, Germany, Great Britain,

---

17 It might be added that Marina Costa Lobo (2008) found that party type made a difference. For the electoral success of mass parties, leaders had relatively little importance, while the leaders of catch-all parties mattered more. Her evidence was, however, entirely cross-sectional.

Netherlands, Norway and Sweden) covering a time period of maximally thirty-seven years (Germany) and minimally twelve years (Netherlands). The authors address three research questions:

- Do voters today more than in the past vote for the party of the leader they like?
- Do leadership evaluations matter more today than in the past when other important influences on voting behaviour are controlled for?
- Has the indirect influence of leaders increased so that party evaluations have become increasingly influenced by voters' evaluations of leaders?

The answer to the first question is that voters indeed vote for the party whose leader they like. However, nothing indicates a secular increase in this correlation (Curtice and Holmberg 2005: 241–3). In order to answer the second question, the authors control for social class, religion, church attendance, left-right position, party identification and party evaluation. Their conclusion is that the independent effect of leader evaluations, where it can be discerned at all, is very limited. Moreover, this effect shows no increase over time (ibid.: 245–6). Finally, the third question is based on the idea that party leaders may shape parties to match their own image. If that is the case, the indirect influence of leaders on party choice may be greater than that which statistical analyses might seem to indicate. In order to highlight this question, the authors examine whether voter evaluations of parties and leaders have come to resemble each other more over time. Again, the result is negative: 'Nowhere is there any consistent evidence of an increase' (ibid.: 251). In sum, the results of this study resoundingly speak against the notion of a secular increase in the importance of party leaders.

These studies are complemented by a volume entitled *Leader's Personalities and the Outcomes of Democratic Elections* edited by Anthony King (2003). Although the six cases (USA, Britain, France, Germany, Canada and Russia) presented in the country chapters are not an ideal selection from the point of view of the present book, this study is important since it has elections rather than survey respondents as the basic unit of analysis. The authors of the individual chapters attempt to assess the importance of leaders at various elections, and the comparative summary, by the editor, compiles this evidence in order to detect patterns across cases as well as over time. The main conclusion is that while there are a few cases where leaders made a crucial difference, leaders are normally not decisive for election outcomes. Moreover, there is no temporal pattern indicating that leader effects are becoming more important (King 2003: 213).

A host of studies of a more limited scope could be added to reinforce the impression created by these three comparative analyses, but this is hardly necessary. As far as the role of party leaders for the party choice of voters and the outcome of elections, the systematic evidence runs emphatically counter to the personalisation thesis.

RESEARCH QUESTIONS

While it would be an exaggeration to describe the relationship between leader evaluations and voter choice as a closed chapter, so much basic research with con-current conclusions exists that this cannot be overlooked in the present context. What kinds of questions should be asked given the relative wealth of previous research on this topic?

A perennial problem in much of the survey-based electoral research is the short distance between the dependent variable – what party people vote for – and some of the most important independent variables (party identification, party evalua-tions). The finding that people vote for the party they identify with and/or evaluate positively hardly comes as a surprise to anyone. In both Holmberg and Oscarsson 2004 and Curtice and Holmberg 2005 the effects of leader effects on party choice compete with the effects of party evaluations. In the former study, focus is on the relative explanatory capacity of these two variables. In the latter, party evaluations are controlled for along with party identification and several socio-economic and cultural variables. How sensible is it to expect that anything might 'explain' party choice better than party evaluation, as these processes are so close to each other that they are nearly identical? How 'fair' is it to have leader evaluations compete with this factor that seems so close to the dependent variable?

This book does not pretend to be able to provide an answer to these questions. For the sake of clarity it should be stressed that the Holmberg and Oscarsson in particular demonstrate awareness of this problem (2004: 160). Moreover, the most important finding from the point of view of the present analysis – the fact that party leader effects do not increase over time – is beyond dispute. However, to make the picture complete it would be useful to have a longitudinal comparative analysis of party leader effects controlling for the usual socio-economic factors without party evaluation and party identification in the equation. Any temporal patterns that may be discovered in an analysis of this kind are potentially quite interesting. The first aim of the empirical part of this chapter is to provide such an analysis.

The relationship between party leaders and voters is, however, not confined to the question whether leaders decide elections, either at the level of the individual voter or in terms of the national election outcome. These are naturally core ques-tions for the study of personalisation; one might talk of personalisation in the strict sense. But it could be said that the importance of party leaders to the way in which voters think of politics has increased irrespective of the fact that their voting choic-es are in the final analysis mostly conditioned by other factors. This 'personalisa-tion lite' is no less interesting as a social and political phenomenon. This chapter will therefore also make an attempt to shed light on the following questions:

– Are there any trends in the intensity with which voters like or dislike party leaders? Do voters pick extreme alternatives more often than in the past?
– What is the role of party identification apart from the fairly self-evident fact that people tend to like the leader of the party that they identify with? Are there any temporal patterns among non-party identifiers (which is a growing segment of the electorate)?

– Are there any future trends evident in the social characteristics of those who have strong views about leaders? Do young citizens have a special profile in this regard? What about party switchers; do they emphasise the role of leaders more than those who remain loyal to their party?

SIX PARLIAMENTARY DEMOCRACIES, 1961–2001

The *European Voter Database*[18] provides a good empirical basis for further analyses of the importance of party leaders to voters in parliamentary democracies. Taken together, the six national election studies systematised in this data set cover four decades, starting with the 1961 German election study and ending with the National Election Study in Britain in 2001. Although the time span covered by the individual national studies varies and despite the fact that the evidence basically ends where the current millennium starts, the data available are more than sufficient to provide a test of the personalisation thesis. If there has been a consistent trend towards a more pronounced role for party leaders in the electoral politics of parliamentary democracies, it should manifest itself in this impressive set of longitudinal data.

Once again, the primary interest concerns temporal trends. Evidence from several countries is necessary to eliminate the risk that the peculiarities of any single national system dictate the conclusions drawn. The alleged trend towards personalisation should be present in most, if not all countries if personalisation is such a pervasive phenomenon as is frequently suggested. However, the analysis in this chapter does not purport to be a fully-fledged comparative study in the sense that it endeavours to explain similarities and differences across cases. Six cases is too limited a number to allow for conclusions of this kind. Of course, should it turn out that trends in Great Britain or Germany clearly differ from those in Denmark, the Netherlands, Norway and Sweden, it would seem reasonable to assume that differences in electoral systems account for an important part of the variation. In order to really test such an assumption, however, a much larger selection of cases would be necessary. Here, the primary ambition is basically descriptive: has the importance of leaders increased over time?

Explaining party choice

Party leader evaluation and party evaluation are closely interrelated. Using party leader evaluation to explain party choice while controlling for party evaluation tends to result in the finding that leaders do not mean very much while party evaluation is a powerful explanatory factor. In a similar vein, other variables, such as socio-economic indicators, tend to have fairly limited explanatory power when they are tested along with party evaluation. As was stressed above, this is not a very surprising finding. The distance between party evaluation and party choice is so short that it is nearly tautological to say that the former explains the latter.

---

18 My thanks are due to the Central Archive for Empirical Social Research at the University of Cologne for providing access to this database. For details about the base, see Mochmann and Zenk-Möltgen 2005: 309-12.

This section tests the explanatory capacity of party leader evaluations on party choice without controls for party evaluation and party identification. Instead, the question is whether party leader evaluations explain a larger portion of the variation in party choice over time when several socio-economic and structural factors are controlled for. If the explanatory power of party leader evaluation displays an increase over time at the expense of other factors that normally explain portions of the variation in party choice, then this can be interpreted as evidence in favour of the personalisation thesis.

As the focus is on possible change over time, the analysis must be designed so as to provide maximal consistency during the period under study. To begin with, the parties included must be the same for the entire period. Moreover, the operationalisation of the dependent and independent variables must be identical from one observation to the next. If the parties included for the various observation years were to vary, then changes over time might be due to some intrinsic qualities of the parties rather than to changes in the generic role of party leaders. If variables are not operationalised the same way throughout the period, the resulting findings may be pure statistical artefacts.

All of this may seem rather self-evident. Nevertheless, in the real world of empirical analysis it makes some difficult choices necessary. To attain maximal consistency, the analysis was limited to two major parties per country. This is unproblematic for countries like Germany and Great Britain. In the cases of Denmark, the Netherlands and Norway, the same two parties have not consistently been the two largest parties at each election. However, this has nearly always been the case, which is why it was deemed more sensible to limit the analysis to the same two parties irrespective of their electoral fortunes. Consequently, the following parties are included throughout the analysis:

Denmark: Social Democrats and Liberals (*Venstre)*

Germany: Social Democrats and Christian Democrats/Christian Social Union

Great Britain: Labour and Conservatives

Netherlands: Labor Party and Christian Democratic Appeal

Norway: Social Democrats and Conservatives

Sweden: Social Democrats and Conservatives

The dependent variables present no problems. For each of these parties and for each year included in the analysis, a binary variable is included. Its values stand for 'did not vote for the party in question' and 'voted for the party in question', respectively. As for the independent variables, a somewhat different logic than in Curtice and Holmberg's study is applied. Curtice and Holmberg wanted to control for basically the same variables across cases. Since empirical data were not available for all countries at each time point included in their study, controls for individual countries varied over time (see Curtice and Holmberg 2005: 243–345). Moreover, for Great Britain, the central independent variable, leader evaluation, was operationalised in a different way in 1983–1992 than during the rest of the period.

As consistency over time within each case is imperative, the present study has opted for an individual set of variables for each country. All variables are included in the same form for all observation years for a particular country. Those years for which these data are not available are omitted from the analysis. This means, of course, that the analysis does not allow for strict comparisons across cases. In other words, the results should not be interpreted so as to mean that party leader evaluations explain a larger proportion of the variation in country A than in country B. Such differences in explained variance may well be due to the varying controls applied for each country. However, the analysis does allow for judgments as to the development of the explanatory power of leader evaluations over time.

In Table 3.1 the results of a series of logistic regressions are shown. In each of them, the dependent variable measures whether respondents voted for the party in question that particular year.

Table 3.1: The partial impact of party leader evaluations on party choice. Logistic regression coefficients

Denmark

	Social Democrats		Liberals	
	Coefficient	Standard error	Coefficient	Standard error
1971	0.55	0.04	0.82	0.07
1994	0.52	0.04	0.68	0.05
1998	0.59	0.03	0.68	0.04

Controls: Age, education, sex

Germany

	Social Democrats		CDU/CSU	
	Coefficient	Standard error	Coefficient	Standard error
1961	0.32	0.03	0.44	0.03
1965	0.46	0.03	0.49	0.04
1972	0.91	0.06	0.53	0.03
1976	1.00	0.06	0.90	0.05
1980	0.75	0.06	0.78	0.06
1983	0.74	0.05	0.83	0.06
1987	0.52	0.03	0.57	0.03
1990	0.49	0.04	0.92	0.07
1994	0.59	0.03	0.76	0.04
1998	0.40	0.02	0.43	0.03

Controls: Education, region, religion

Great Britain

	Labour		Conservatives	
	Coefficient	Standard error	Coefficient	Standard error
1964	0.89	0.05	0.65	0.06
1970	0.78	0.05	0.72	0.05
1974 (F)	0.47	0.09	0.46	0.08
1974 (O)	0.55	0.10	0.55	0.07
1979	0.60	0.15	0.58	0.18
1997	0.52	0.02	0.52	0.02
2001	0.39	0.10	0.36	0.08

Controls: Education, region, religion

Netherlands

	Labor Party		CDA	
	Coefficient	Standard error	Coefficient	Standard error
1986	0.04	0.00*	0.04	0.00
1989	0.08	0.01	0.07	0.01
1994	0.04	0.00	0.03	0.01
1998	0.05	0.01	0.05	0.01

Controls: Church attendance, education, subjective class identity

* The figures have been rounded off from three decimals. If standard error is given as 0.00, it is less than 0.005

Norway

	Social Democrats		Conservatives	
	Coefficient	Standard error	Coefficient	Standard error
1981	0.07	0.00	0.08	0.01
1985	0.07	0.00	0.07	0.00
1989	0.07	0.00	0.06	0.00
1993	0.05	0.00	0.06	0.00
1997	0.05	0.00	0.07	0.00

Controls: Church attendance, education, region

Sweden

	Social Democrats		Conservatives	
	Coefficient	Standard error	Coefficient	Standard error
1979	0.73	0.03	0.72	0.04
1982	0.61	0.03	0.77	0.04
1985	0.63	0.03	0.82	0.04
1988	0.66	0.03	0.75	0.04
1991	0.65	0.03	0.74	0.04
1994	0.70	0.03	0.72	0.04
1998	0.56	0.03	0.83	0.05

Controls: Education, sex, urbanisation

Table 3.1 conveys a fairly straightforward impression: the data do not support the hypothesis that the importance of leader evaluations for party choice has grown over time when other factors are controlled for. In most cases, there seems to be no secular trend at all. For Great Britain, leader evaluations seem to explain somewhat less of the variation in party choice towards the end of the period. For Germany, the impact of leader evaluations peaked in the 1970s but has become somewhat weaker and less consistent since then. Overall, the results clearly confirm the negative conclusion drawn by Curtice and Holmberg.

The intensity of leader evaluations
If party leaders as individuals have come to mean more to voters over time, one might expect that voters examine leaders more thoroughly and form firmer opinions about them than in the past. In other words, it did not matter that much earlier what kind of person led one's favourite party, it was still one's favourite party. Today, by contrast, voters are supposed to be much more influenced by their impressions of party leaders than in the past. Therefore, one would expect them to have much clearer and more intense views of party leaders than earlier.

Many electoral surveys have, for quite some time, asked respondents to rank their sympathies for party leaders. The *European Voter Database* includes an eleven-grade measure where respondents rank leaders on a thermometer scale from a very negative evaluation over a neutral position all the way to a very positive evaluation. The interesting question in the present context is whether voters during more recent years tend to pick extreme alternatives (a high degree of dislike or sympathy) more often than earlier. Again, if such a consistent trend is to be found, this would speak in favour of the personalisation thesis.

In order to examine this question, party leader evaluations for the two parties included for each country were combined into a party leader evaluation scale. This scale measures the intensity, not the direction of party leader evaluations. In other words, the question is not whether voters like or dislike a given party leader, but how intensely they like or dislike him or her. The value 0 means that a respondent has a neutral view of both party leaders; the value 5 indicates that a respondent likes or dislikes both party leaders intensely. Table 3.2 shows how the mean values of this measure have evolved over the years.

Table 3.2: The intensity of party leader evaluations. Mean values, scale from 0 to 5

Denmark

	Mean	N
1971	2.76	1225
1973	2.96	508
1994	2.54	1048
1998	2.64	1982

Germany

	Mean	N
1961	2.73	1240
1965	2.93	1240
1972	3.27	1215
1976	2.95	1182
1980	3.01	995
1983	2.61	1008
1987	2.72	1529
1990	2.84	886
1994	2.52	2034
1998	2.56	1949

Great Britain

	Mean	N
1964	1.28	1769
1966	1.42	1874
1970	1.33	1843
1974 (F)*	2.47	2408
1974 (O)	2.35	2337
1979	2.16	1818
1997	2.62	2965
2001	2.26	2904

* Two elections were held in 1974, one in February and another in October

Netherlands

	Mean	N
1986	2.57	1587
1989	2.47	1501
1994	2.36	1775
1998	2.06	1664

Norway

	Mean	N
1981	2.40	1515
1985	2.39	2088
1989	2.23	2123
1993	2.21	2121
1997	1.81	1966

Sweden

	Mean	N
1979	3.06	2623
1982	2.85	2645
1985	2.91	2611
1988	2.60	2452
1991	2.52	2423
1994	2.69	2256
1998	2.57	2057

The analysis reveals much more continuity than change in the intensity of party leader evaluations. The only clear change would seem to occur in Britain between 1970 and 1974. Up until 1970, the intensity of party leader evaluations was low in Britain. From the mid-1970s on, it has been on the same general level as in the five other countries included in the database. Apart from this finding, what little change there is certainly does not speak in favour of the personalisation thesis. In the Netherlands and in Norway the intensity of leader evaluations has declined linearly, but the magnitude of change is modest. Sweden shares a similar pattern, although the change is not entirely linear. Basically, however, the result of this analysis is that little has changed in the intensity of party leader evaluations during recent decades.

Party identification and leader evaluations

A classical difference between Western European and US research on parties and elections has to do with the European emphasis on socio-economic and structural factors and the American focus on party identification. Largely inspired by the Lipset-Rokkan cleavage model, European researchers have primarily used factors such as social class and cultural diversity to account for party formation and citizens' political affiliations. In the USA, such factors have assumed somewhat less importance. Instead, what is known as the Michigan model of electoral analysis has focused on the psychological affinity that individual citizens feel towards a given party. A large share of the American people has been found to have a permanent or long-standing attachment to either of the two main parties. Party identification has a specific and independent role when Americans orient themselves in the political world. Traditionally, Europeans too have had strong party identifications. In Europe, however, party identification has largely been a function of the socio-economic and cultural factors that condition people's attachment to political parties. For many decades, therefore, the independent role of party identification as an explanatory factor was limited in Europe (Berglund *et al* 2005: 106–7).

What makes the question of party identification interesting in the present context is the fact that partisanship among European voters has declined over the past decades. The patterns and rapidity of the change have varied from country to country, but 'the overall downward trend is unmistakable' (Dalton 2002: 26). In the 1950s and 1960s, most West Europeans clearly identified with a given political party, and many were strong adherents of their favourite party. Today, nonidentifiers form the largest group, and strong party identifiers are a small minority among the electorate (ibid.: 27; Berglund *et al* 2005: 110).

Although there have been signs of a concomitant decline in electoral turnout (Aarts and Wessels 2005: 66–7), the decline in party identifications has clearly been more marked and linear. This means that more citizens without a party identification make choices concerning parties and candidates today than in the past. The question examined in this section is whether the degree of party identification has a bearing on how intensely voters like or dislike political leaders and if there has been any change in this regard over time. Do non-party identifiers more readily pick extreme alternatives when asked about their view of party leaders? To the extent that party-identifiers and non-identifiers differ from each other, have these differences changed over time?

In order to examine these questions, a series of regressions were run for each of the six countries using the party leader evaluation scale presented above as dependent variable. The independent variables were either three or four-point scales based on interview questions about whether respondents identified with a given party and how strong this identification was. The value 0 stands for no party identification, the highest value (2 or 3) for strong identification. The variable does not measure the direction of party identification (what party a respondent identifies with), only its strength. The question is, in other words, whether voters with weak or non-existent party identifications view the leaders of the two main parties differently than do citizens who have clear or strong party identifications.

Table 3.3: *The impact of the strength of party identification on the intensity of party leader evaluations (combined values for two main parties). OLS regression*

Denmark

	B	Standard error	Significance
1973	0.19	0.05	0.001
1994	0.16	0.04	0.000
1998	0.17	0.03	0.000

Germany

	B	Standard error	Significance
1961	0.38	0.07	0.000
1972	0.38	0.03	0.000
1976	0.28	0.03	0.000
1980	0.20	0.04	0.000
1983	0.19	0.04	0.000
1987	0.25	0.04	0.000
1990	0.23	0.04	0.000
1994	0.34	0.03	0.000
1998	0.19	0.03	0.000

Great Britain

	B	Standard error	Significance
1964	0.08	0.02	0.000
1966	0.13	0.02	0.000
1970	0.11	0.02	0.000
1974 (F)	0.43	0.03	0.000
1974 (O)	0.39	0.03	0.000
1979	0.27	0.03	0.000
1997	0.51	0.04	0.000
2001	0.58	0.04	0.000

Netherlands

	B	Standard error	Significance
1986	0.24	0.04	0.000
1989	0.17	0.04	0.000
1994	0.18	0.04	0.000
1998	0.19	0.03	0.000

Norway

	B	Standard error	Significance
1981	0.41	0.04	0.000
1985	0.37	0.03	0.000
1989	0.34	0.03	0.000
1993	0.27	0.03	0.000
1997	0.17	0.02	0.000

Sweden

	B	Standard error	Significance
1979	0.50	0.03	0.000
1982	0.47	0.02	0.000
1985	0.48	0.02	0.000
1988	0.52	0.02	0.000
1991	0.40	0.02	0.000
1994	0.41	0.03	0.000
1998	0.32	0.03	0.000

The association between the strength of party identification and the intensity of party leader evaluations is positive. Citizens with marked party identities are more prone to like or dislike party leaders more intensely than citizens with weak or no party identities. In Denmark and in the Netherlands, this difference has been relatively stable over the years. In Norway and Sweden it has declined slightly, whereas the opposite seems to be the case with Britain. In Germany, finally, there has been some fluctuation in the explanatory power of party identification.

Overall, however, the message in Table 3.3 is straightforward. The idea that non-identifiers focus more strongly on the party leaders and consequently tend to have stronger views about them receives no support in the empirical evidence at hand. Intense evaluations of party leaders seem to be more of a function of partisanship than of its absence.

Age and party leader evaluations
'Age, one of the most fundamental predictors of political participation, has long been found to influence electoral turnout as well as patterns of party membership, involvement in voluntary organizations, and engagement in group activity', Pippa Norris writes in a highly-acclaimed overview of research on political participation (2002: 89). And although it has proven to be difficult to determine exactly to what extent the correlation between age and political behaviour reflects a generation effect, a period effect or a life cycle effect (Jennings and Niemi 1981: 119–20; Wass 2008: 30–4), the impact of age has been found to be robust. Basically, the pattern is that participation in elections and other forms of 'conventional' political activity rises with age, while alternative forms of political participation display a negative correlation with age (Bengtsson 2008: 105, 149–59). While this might seem to

support the idea that the 'postmaterialist generation' takes a different view of politics than older cohorts of citizens, there have been signs that the differences among age groups are not stable and in fact may be diminishing over time (Topf 1998: 70–1). Age makes a difference as to how citizens view politics, but the differences between younger, middle-aged and older citizens are not static but dynamic in a longer perspective.

If the personalisation of politics is part of a larger process of postmodernisation brought about by the structural transformation of society and the revolution in communication technology, then one would expect younger generations of citizens to have a more personalised view of politics than older citizens. It is the younger voters, after all, who have grown up in a period marked by weakening structural cleavages and the self-evident dominance of television as a channel of political communication. On the other hand, one would not expect the impact of age to be stable over longer periods of time. With the passage of time, a growing part of the electorate belongs to the segment of the population that has spent its formative years in a post-industrial society.

To examine these questions, a series of regression analyses were run with age as the independent variable and the intensity of party leader evaluations as the independent variable. Table 3.4 shows the results of these tests.

Table 3.4:   *The impact of age on the intensity of party leader evaluations.*
OLS regression

Denmark

	B	Standard error	Significance
1971	0.08	0.02	0.001
1994	0.05	0.02	0.017
1998	0.03	0.01	0.003

Germany

	B	Standard error	Significance
1961	0.05	0.01	0.000
1965	0.02	0.01	0.063
1972	0.03	0.00*	0.106
1976	0.01	0.00	0.013
1980	0.01	0.00	0.004
1983	0.01	0.00	0.000
1987	0.01	0.00	0.001
1990	0.02	0.00	0.000
1994	0.00	0.00	0.176
1998	0.01	0.00	0.000

*   The figures have been rounded off from three decimals. If standard error is given as 0.00, it is less than 0.005

Great Britain

	B	Standard error	Significance
1964	-0.00	0.00	0.153
1966	0.00	0.00	0.538
1970	0.00	0.00	0.012
1974 (F)	0.01	0.00	0.000
1974 (O)	0.01	0.00	0.000
1979	0.01	0.00	0.000
1997	0.01	0.00	0.000
2001	0.01	0.00	0.000

Netherlands

	B	Standard error	Significance
1986	0.01	0.00	0.000
1989	0.02	0.00	0.000
1994	0.01	0.00	0.000
1998	0.01	0.00	0.000

Norway

	B	Standard error	Significance
1981	0.01	0.00	0.000
1985	0.01	0.00	0.000
1989	0.01	0.00	0.000
1993	0.01	0.00	0.000
1997	0.01	0.00	0.000

Sweden

	B	Standard error	Significance
1979	0.10	0.02	0.000
1982	0.06	0.01	0.000
1985	0.07	0.02	0.000
1988	0.10	0.02	0.000
1991	0.10	0.01	0.000
1994	0.09	0.02	0.000
1998	0.06	0.02	0.000

Table 3.4 conveys a monotonous impression. The impact of age on the intensity of party leader evaluations is limited indeed. Moreover, to the extent that variation in age affects party leader at all, the association is positive. Older rather than younger voters tend to have intense likes or dislikes for party leaders. As the impact of age is so limited, this observation should not be emphasised too much. Far more important in the present context is the fact that there is considerably more continuity than change in the relationship between age and leader evaluations over time. True, the association has become slightly weaker in the cases of Denmark and Germany. Still, this limited change is insufficient to support any conclusion in favour of the expectations about the effects of the age factor. It is quite apparently not the young voters who have particularly strong views about political leaders, and nothing indicates that a change has been under way in this regard.

PARTY SWITCHERS AND PARTY LEADERS

As the structurally-determined entrenchment of party alignments among the electorate has waned, the propensity of voters to switch parties from one election to the next has increased. True, the levels of electoral volatility vary greatly among the established democracies. Still, as comparative research over extended periods of time has demonstrated: '[T]he direction of change is clearly uniform. There is an increasing tendency for voters to report that they shifted their votes between elections, especially in nations where the declines in partisan attachments have been greater' (Dalton *et al* 2002: 44). There are more 'floating voters' today than in the past, and in many democracies party switchers are numerous enough to decide any election.

Are those voters who remain loyal to their party different from party switchers when it comes to the intensity of party leader evaluation? Inherent in much of the theorising on the personalisation of politics is the notion that it is the citizens with weaker ties to traditional collective loyalties that focus on person rather than party:

> With weaker partisan loyalties, and in the absence of strong social links to specific parties, such as class or religion, voters are more likely to switch their vote between elections, or to abstain. In these circumstances, weaker voter attachments to parties should enhance the role of the leader in both the mobilization and conversion of the vote. In the absence of party cues, voters will rely more heavily on the appeal of the candidates' personalities in order to decide their vote.
>
> McAllister 2007: 582

If this is the case, one would expect party switchers rather than party loyalists to pay more attention to party leaders and their qualities when making voting decisions. This, in turn, might affect the intensity with which they view party leaders. Table 3.5 shows the mean values of the party leader evaluation scale for party switchers and party loyalists. This distinction is based on whether respondents voted for the same party in the previous election. Admittedly, this is a rather crude operationalisation as it is based on two elections only; in the present context, however, it is the only practically feasible solution.

Table 3.5: *Vote switching and the intensity of party leader evaluations. Mean values for selected years*

Denmark

	Voted for same party	Voted for different party	
	Mean	Mean	N
1971	2.84	2.57	981
1973	3.03	2.69	470
1994	2.63	2.53	837
1998	2.76	2.50	1644

Germany

	Voted for same party	Voted for different party	
	Mean	Mean	N
1965	3.02	2.89	938
1972	3.34	3.16	955
1976	3.06	2.95	922
1980	3.12	2.80	810
1983	2.68	2.50	912
1987	2.86	2.48	1103
1990	2.88	2.80	760
1994	2.74	2.40	1265

Great Britain

	Voted for same party	Voted for different party	
	Mean	Mean	N
1964	1.29	1.25	1769
1966	1.46	1.36	1874
1970	1.41	1.24	1843
1974 (F)	2.60	2.31	2408
1974 (O)	2.41	2.25	2337
1979	2.20	2.10	1818
1997	2.83	2.39	2965
2001	2.50	1.96	1424

Netherlands

	Voted for same party	Voted for different party	
	Mean	Mean	N
1986	2.69	2.42	1091
1989	2.54	2.31	1232
1994	2.45	2.23	1182
1998	2.13	2.04	1210

Norway

	Voted for same party	Voted for different party	
	Mean	Mean	N
1981	2.57	2.31	502
1985	2.53	2.19	1532
1989	2.40	2.09	1529
1993	2.29	2.26	1482
1997	1.87	1.76	1506

Sweden

	Voted for same party	Voted for different party	
	Mean	Mean	N
1979	3.23	2.88	2131
1982	3.01	2.77	2080
1985	3.09	2.69	2045
1988	2.82	2.25	1766
1991	2.74	2.44	1511
1994	2.92	2.53	1433
1998	2.74	2.50	1220

Table 3.5 repeats a pattern which is familiar by now. It is not party switchers who tend to take strong views on party leaders. Quite the contrary: those who stay with their party consistently display higher values of the party leader evaluation scale than party switchers. The differences are not dramatic but they are clear enough to be statistically significant for most of the cases. Moreover, there is no temporal pattern indicating that the differences are diminishing over time. With few exceptions, they remain on the same general level throughout the period examined. To the extent that one expects electoral volatility to contribute to a stronger focus on party leaders, the data in Table 3.5 offer little evidence to support this notion.

SUMMARY AND CONCLUSIONS

With the aid of the *European Voter Database* (six countries, 1961–2001), this chapter has attempted to highlight the following questions:

- Has the importance of party leader evaluations for party choice increased when several socio-economic and cultural factors are controlled for?
- Have there been any temporal trends in the intensity with which voters like or dislike party leaders on a thermometer scale?
- Have waning party identifications led to more intensity in the way voters view party leaders?
- How does age affect the way voters view party leaders?
- How does party switching affect the way voters view party leaders?

The results of the empirical analysis provide reasonably clear answers to each of these questions:

- The importance of party leader evaluations for party choice has not increased over time
- Voters display no tendency to have more intense opinions about party leaders over time
- It is not voters with weak or no party identification who focus more on party leaders by liking or disliking them more intensely, in fact it is the other way round
- The explanatory power of age vis-à-vis the intensity of party leader evaluations is limited; to the extent there are differences, it is the older, rather than the younger, voters who have strong preferences
- It is the party loyalists rather than party switchers who have strong preferences regarding party leaders

The chief objective of this chapter has been to provide answers about trends over time. The main conclusion must be formulated in a negative way; nothing in the evidence surveyed suggests that the importance of party leaders has grown. To this conclusion, a second important observation should be added. The analysis strongly suggests that the party leader factor is, by and large, a function of the party factor. Party leaders are first and foremost associated with their parties, and it is the voters' evaluation of the party that is the strongest determinant of their evaluation of a given leader. If a certain party is important to a voter, he tends to have strong views about various party leaders. If parties matter less to a citizen he is less prone to harbour strong sentiments about party leaders.

The results of this chapter provide additional perspectives and evidence to the work presented by, first and foremost, Curtice, Holmberg and Oscarsson. The present analysis essentially goes to support their conclusions.

chapter four | how politics is presented: media and personalisation

The power of autonomous media is creating new rules for democratic practice

Swanson and Mancini 1996a, 274

A study of the personalisation of politics can hardly avoid addressing the role of the media in this process. In fact, many would probably argue that the media should be at the centre of attention in this regard. It would be difficult to picture the rise to prominence of the personalisation thesis without major changes in the media landscape surrounding politics. For more than half a century, mass media have been the main arena of politics. Traditional forms of political communication, such as public meetings, door-to-door canvassing and stump tours, have by no means vanished from the scene. Still, it is fair to say that most political communication has for many decades been mediated rather than direct. Second, the predominance of television has profoundly affected the conditions for political communication. Political actors, as well as traditional news media, have been compelled to adjust to a setting where the special features of televised communication occupy the centre stage. Mass communication has not been the same after the advent of television. Moreover, throughout the media sector, processes of professionalisation and commercialisation have had pervasive effects. The influence of governments and political parties over newspapers and broadcasting has declined. Today, the bulk of the media sector closely guards its status as an autonomous actor in society with the task of providing independent and critical coverage of political actors, institutions and processes (McAllister 2007: 578–82; Swanson and Mancini 1996b: 14–20).

The increased importance of broadcasting and politically independent major newspapers has presented a major challenge to parties and candidates throughout the postwar period. An ever smaller portion of political communication is controlled by parties and candidates themselves; to an increasing degree, they have had to adjust to conditions determined by the media. True, they can present themselves in the media without journalistic interventions by purchasing advertisements in newspapers as well as on radio and television. Moreover, the advent of the Internet and of other forms of new media technology has provided entirely new arenas of political communication. The traditional formats offered by newspapers and broadcasting are increasingly challenged by multiple channels, many of which are interactive in character (Strandberg 2006). Still, the press and television retain their central position as sources of political information and arenas for electoral campaigns. Data on the 2007 Finnish parliamentary election can be used to illustrate this. Finland is a technologically-advanced country with a high level of Internet penetration. Still, 65 per cent of the respondents in the 2007 Finnish Election Study had not followed election reporting on the Internet at all. Three quarters of the respondents had never visited home pages of parties or candidates, and 87 per cent had never visited candidates' Internet diaries or blogs. By contrast, merely 6 per cent had not followed election news coverage on television at all. Seventeen per cent had refrained totally from watching party leader interviews and debates on television, and 13 per cent had not read any newspaper election coverage. Overall, television and newspapers still occupy the centre stage as campaign arenas.

The present study wants to highlight the question whether politics today presents itself in a more personalised way than during earlier periods. This is an objective which is as important as it is difficult to achieve. On the one hand, any attempt to assess the personalisation of politics without analysing how politics is presented would seem quite insufficient. To many people, the personalisation of politics is in fact something that takes place in the media. On the other hand, it is a topic that should be approached in a variety of ways that are difficult to cover in a single study. Moreover, as media, especially television, are frequently seen as a central cause of personalisation, there is also a risk of circular reasoning in this area. In addition, studies of media and campaign content are quite challenging since they require analyses of large bodies of data in the form of texts, images, sounds and films. To perform such studies both over time and with comparisons across cases is demanding indeed.

As is evident from the Introduction of this book, media-oriented research so far is inconclusive when it comes to the extent of personalisation in stable parliamentary democracies. Clearly, some studies point to a more or less linear development towards more personalisation. In many cases, however, different studies have produced conflicting results. In quite a few instances, in fact, substantial evidence against the personalisation thesis has been presented. One particular problem in this research is the lack of comparative studies. The comparative study of media content is difficult because content analyses are always rather cumbersome; linguistic and other practical obstacles contribute to the relative scarcity of such studies as well.

The present chapter approaches these questions from the following points of departure. First, using material from television is ruled out because television, due to its intrinsic focus on individuals rather than abstract issues, is seen as one of the chief factors behind personalisation. If it is true that television automatically focuses on persons, then evidence for personalisation based on the way television presents politics has a circular ring to it. Of course, the way television presents issues and people has not remained static over the years – far from it. Still, it seems warranted to exclude this type of evidence from our survey.

Second, it is important that the empirical analysis include both journalistic material and features that parties and politicians themselves control. Politics is, to a large extent, filtered through the journalistic choices made by reporters and editorial staffs before it is presented to the audience. Still, parties and politics have important channels that they can use to reach voters without using reporters as mediators. The analysis in this book seeks to provide answers about possible personalisation in both forms of political presentation.

Finally, it is necessary that the channels of communication where evidence for and against the personalisation thesis is sought be fairly constant over time. There should preferably be no such structural and functional changes in the channels themselves that might constitute explanations of why personalisation looks different at $t+1$ than it did at t.

For these reasons, daily newspapers will be used as the source of empirical data for this study. Admittedly, newspapers are today somewhat less important as a vehicle for political communication than half a century ago. Nevertheless, the press continues to play a central role in politics. From a technical and functional point of view, it has changed relatively little, which is a methodological advantage in the present context.

The empirical analysis in this chapter highlights the personalisation of politics in the media in three ways. Focus is once again on leaders and candidates. The first study is based on Ana Inés Langer's dissertation (2006) on British prime ministers 1945–1999 supplemented with new primary evidence relating to Gordon Brown. This analysis largely represents the routine treatment of political leaders, as the empirical evidence originates from periods between election campaigns. The second analysis draws on Bengt Johansson's work (2008) on Swedish media coverage of parliamentary elections. In these data, party leaders are portrayed in media in the midst of election campaigns. Finally, the third study tells something about possible changes in the way parties and candidates wish to be portrayed. An analysis of party and candidate advertisements in Finland's largest daily newspaper in 1962–2007 gives an idea of the relative visibility of parties as compared to candidates over the years.

BRITAIN: PRIME MINISTERS IN *THE TIMES*

Langer's 2006 dissertation at the London School of Economics and Political Science consists of a longitudinal overview and an intensive case study focused on Tony Blair. The present analysis is based on the former part of Langer's study. Her analysis covers British prime ministers from 1945 until 1999 with the exception of Anthony Eden, Alec Douglas-Home and James Callaghan who served too briefly to meet the criteria for inclusion in Langer's study. Consequently, the following prime ministers were included in her study: Clement Attlee, Winston Churchill, Harold Macmillan, Harold Wilson, Edward Heath, Margaret Thatcher, John Major and Tony Blair.

In empirical terms, Langer examines how these British prime ministers are covered in *The Times*, one of England's leading dailies.[19] For each of them, two-week periods from their first three years in office were included: for the first year, the first two weeks in November; for the second year, the second and third

---

19 Langer has summarized large portions of her data in Langer 2007. Here, however, her unpublished dissertation has been used as source.

week in November; for the third year, the third and fourth week in November. Consequently, the periods include what might be called normal coverage of the prime ministers; they do not cover election campaigns. All articles, except people/ obituaries sections, advertising, letters to the Editor, indexes and Court Circulars were included in the study (Langer 2006: 286).

It was not possible to supplement Langer's analysis with more recent data in exactly the same way that she had done for the eight Prime Ministers in 1945– 1999. Tony Blair was replaced by Gordon Brown as party leader and prime minister in June 2007. As the supplementary analysis was conducted in late 2008, a third year for Gordon Brown is not available for empirical analysis. It was decided to include only the second year in office for Gordon Brown. A three-week period in November (the last three weeks) 2008 was analysed for Gordon Brown using the same methods as in Langer's study.

Three aspects studied by Langer are included in the present analysis: the overall visibility of prime ministers, references to their leadership qualities, and the use of personal as opposed to formal terms when referring to prime ministers.

The overall visibility of prime ministers is of course a central indicator of the personalisation of politics. If the political importance of individual leaders has increased over the years one would expect them to figure more prominently in the media. As Langer puts it, 'the leader increasingly becomes the main public face of the party and the cabinet and becomes more known and familiar as their presence in the public domain increases (Foley 1993; Mughan 2000)' (p. 120). Langer studied overall visibility by calculating the number of articles that mentioned the incumbent prime minister, the share of those articles of all articles published, and the number of times the incumbent prime minister was mentioned per 10,000 words in *The Times*. These calculations gave similar results. The absolute number of references to the prime minister displayed a somewhat stronger trend than the relative share of articles mentioning the incumbent. This was due to the overall growth of the number of articles in *The Times* during the period under study. The present analysis limits itself to the relative share of articles that mention the incumbent prime minister.

Figure 4.1 shows the percentage of articles that refer to the incumbent prime minister either by name or position. A total of 21,896 articles during the period 1945–2008 were examined.[20] Of these, 843 or 3.9 per cent contained references to the prime minister. Articles that discuss the office of the prime minister as a general constitutional matter with no reference to the person occupying the office were omitted.

The trend displayed by Figure 4.1 is not entirely linear. There was first a slight decline from Attlee to Macmillan. When Harold Wilson assumed office, the percentage of articles dealing with the Prime Minister clearly increased, only to decline again with Edward Heath. Starting with Margaret Thatcher the percentage has been over 4, with Gordon Brown in 2008 representing a clear peak. Overall,

---

20 The number of articles examined for Gordon Brown in 2008 was 2877.

the change is not particularly marked. A growth from a little over 3 per cent to a little less than 6 per cent does seem to point to increased visibility for prime ministers over time, but it is hardly appropriate to speak of a dramatic development.

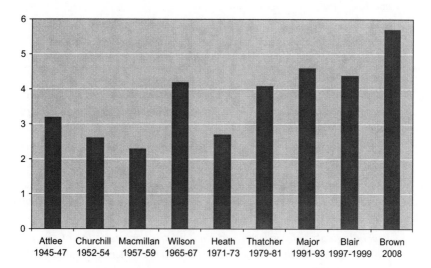

Figure 4.1: Percentage of articles in *The Times* mentioning the Prime Ministers

Sources: For 1945–1997, Langer 2006: 122; for 2008, author's own analysis

All things considered, however, the relative visibility of prime ministers has increased more than these percentages would seem to indicate. It should be borne in mind that they were calculated on the basis of articles in all sections of *The Times*. The main areas of growth in the paper have been the sports, entertainment and human interest sections. For instance, Langer notes that the sports section 'grew from 30 articles per week in 1945 to 298 articles per week in 1999, representing 5 and 16 per cent respectively of the total number of stories in *The Times*' (p. 123). It is, of course, highly unlikely that the prime minister should figure in articles in these sections. Consequently, political coverage in *The Times* has been reduced in relative terms. Had the analysis been limited to 'politically relevant' sections of the paper, the growth pattern would in all likelihood have been much more marked.[21]

Leadership qualities were defined as "personality traits that have a direct link to a leader's capability for governing" (Langer 2006: 129). The following excerpt from Langer's Coding Frame shows what kinds of personality traits are included:

---

21 The reason why this was not done was that Langer's study to an important extent dealt with the politicisation of the prime minister's private persona. Therefore, all sections of the paper were potentially relevant to her work.

1. *Integrity: references to honesty, decency, trustworthiness, integrity, etc. or their opposites.*

2. *Strength: references to his/her strength, courage, power, determination etc. or lack of thereof in regard to the party, other politicians, other leaders or public opinion.*

3. *Charisma: references to the public appeal or popularity or lack thereof of his/her leadership grounded on unspecific leadership qualities (i.e. not because of the popularity of the government policies or the party or his/her private qualities).*

4. *Competence: references to his/her leadership skills for performing as prime minister, including ability as statesman and past political experiences/performances.*

5. *Intelligence: references to his/her 'brain power' or lack thereof to understand or solve issues, to come up with fresh solutions, etc.*

6. *Communication and rhetorical skills: references to the quality or lack thereof of his/her performances in Parliament, the media, and/or in other public realms.*

7. *Psychological: references to psychological characteristics of the prime minister's personality that are clearly linked to his/her leadership qualities (e.g. control freak).*

8. *Political/personal: references to leadership qualities that touch upon his/ her personal life or the 'image' of it.[22]*

Figure 4.2 shows the share of articles containing references to leadership qualities as percentages of all articles that referred to the incumbent prime minister.

Between 1945 and 1999, references to leadership qualities largely repeat the pattern that was found for overall visibility in Figure 4.1. The percentages are generally speaking fairly low. There is an increased frequency for Wilson, a decline for Heath and a growth starting with Thatcher. Langer mentions two noteworthy changes towards the end of the period studied by her. In addition to traditional leadership qualities – various aspects of political competence – new kinds of references started to appear. Some of them referred to psychological features of a leader's personality: 'bully', 'control freak' and so on (Langer 2006: 130). Others referred to the image of leaders as individuals. These can of course be regarded as nonpolitical; in fact, they can also be used so as to define the political leadership of prime ministers. Thus, John Major who had 'traded so far on *being Mr Nice Guy*' could use this image as a tool for his leadership as well (ibid.: 131, italics in original). By the same token, Tony Blair's participation in a World Summit for Children was connected to his '*image as a caring family man*' (ibid.).

---

22 Excerpted from Langer 2006: 289-90. Langer's Coding Frame was adapted from Wattenberg 1991.

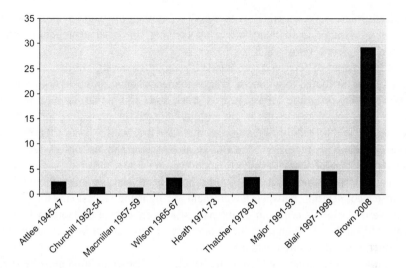

Figure 4.2: Articles referring to leadership qualities as percentage of all articles that mention the Prime Ministers

Sources: For 1945–1997, Langer 2006: 129–32; for 2008, author's own analysis

The second change noted by Langer is the growth in negative references. Throughout the first half of the period she studied, most references to leadership qualities were positive in tone:

> '[U]ntil relatively recently, features of the Prime Ministers' leadership qualities tended to be mentioned more for praise than for scrutiny' (p. 133). Starting with Thatcher, the frequency of negative references began to grow; for Blair, no less than 40 per cent of the references to leadership qualities were negative (p. 132).

With Gordon Brown in 2008, references to leadership qualities reach an entirely new level. Almost 30 per cent of the articles that mention him refer to his leadership qualities. These references dealt with a wide variety of aspects: competence, psychological characteristics, communication skills etc. Many of them were clearly commending in tone. His leadership could be characterised as marked by 'efficiency' (Nov. 15, 2008, p. 39). He could be described as 'a leader of global stature' (Nov. 22, 19) or as 'the best leader... to deal with Britain's economy in recession' (Nov. 28, 5). On the other hand, negative references to Brown's leadership qualities were frequent, too: 'The strategy has backfired' (Nov. 29, 17); 'Never has government strategy been so counter-intuitive' (Nov. 29, 19). His communications skills could also be the subject of criticism: 'The voters will... tire of the Prime Minister's superhero rhetoric' (Nov. 22, 29); or he could be described as being 'more interested in grabbing eco-headlines than doing anything real for the environment' (Nov. 28, 31). From a psychological point of view, his leadership could be described as 'assured' or marked by 'confidence' (Nov. 15, 39). A less benign commentary talked about 'unashamed self-confidence bordering on impudence' (Nov. 18, 8).

The upsurge of references to leadership qualities during Gordon Brown can scarcely be attributed to a general and permanent change in the style of journalistic reporting on prime ministers. It is much more likely that the high frequency of these references is due to the political conditions prevailing in Britain in November 2008. Britain, like much of the industrial world, was in the midst of a severe economic recession. The Brown government had just introduced an extensive package of special economic measures to counter the crisis. A few weeks earlier, Gordon Brown had also figured prominently on the international scene to foster cooperation between governments to fight the recession. This activity, and the opposition's criticism of it, sparked a lively debate on Gordon Brown's leadership style. The high percentage of references to leadership qualities in 2008 largely reflects these circumstances.

While the exceptionally high figure for Gordon Brown in 2008 must be attributed to special circumstances, it nevertheless does not gainsay the conclusion that references to leadership qualities have become more common over time.

Finally, the way prime ministers were referred to in *The Times* texts was investigated. The aim was to find out whether there has been a movement toward a more personal and intimate style of reporting concerning prime ministers. One way of measuring this is to calculate the occurrence of personal terms as opposed to formal and impersonal terms used to refer to prime ministers. 'Prime Minister' and Mr/Mrs plus last name were classified as impersonal terms. First plus last name, last name only and first name only were classified as personal terms. For all articles containing references to the incumbent prime minister the occurrence of personal terms of reference was registered. If an article contained several of the above-mentioned terms, it was classified according to the 'most personal' term used to refer to the prime minister. The occurrence of personal terms was registered separately for the headline and the body of the article (see Langer's Coding Frame, Langer 2006, 288). Figure 4.3 demonstrates how the use of personal terms has evolved over time.

A formal or 'impersonal' style of reference was predominant until Thatcher's period as Prime Minister. The normal way of referring to them was "Prime Minister" or, for instance, "Mr. Heath". By the 1990s, the personal style of reference had become entirely dominant. Nine out of ten references today are of the personal kind. By far the most common way to refer to a prime minister is to use both first and last name ("Tony Blair", "Gordon Brown"). In other words, the way newspapers refer to a prime minister today is identical with the usage concerning ordinary people. Even more familiar references occur now and then: the Prime Minister can be referred to simply as 'Gordon' (Nov. 13, 2008, p. 10) or even, playfully, as 'Santa Brown' (Nov. 19, 33) or 'Super-Gordo' (Nov. 20, 31). All of this demonstrates that a much more familiar tone of reporting is considered *comme-il-faut* today. Prime ministers appear not only as institutions but as persons.

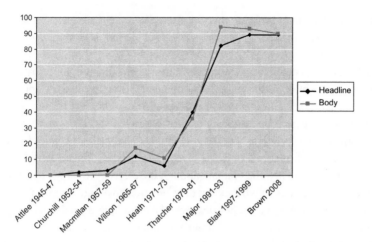

Figure 4.3: Percentage of articles mentioning the Prime Ministers that refer to them using 'personal' terms

Sources: For 1945–1997, Langer 2006: 141; for 2008, author's own analysis

In sum, the data on how British prime ministers are portrayed in one of England's leading dailies seems to support the idea of a personalisation of political reporting. The overall visibility of prime ministers has grown; references to their leadership qualities have become more common; and they are today referred to in clearly more personal terms than three decades ago.

SWEDEN: PARTY LEADERS, ELECTION CAMPAIGNS AND THE PRESS

The Department of Journalism and Mass Communication (JMG) at Göteborg University has been conducting content analyses of mass media in connection with national election campaigns in Sweden since 1979. The research carried out within its Media Election Studies programme focuses on press and television news in the last four weeks of each election campaign. All political content in the three largest morning papers in Sweden (*Dagens Nyheter, Göteborgs-Posten* and *Svenska Dagbladet*) is analysed along with two tabloid papers with a nationwide circulation (*Aftonbladet* and *Expressen*). Moreover, corresponding analyses of news programmes on television are carried out; these will, however, not be included here.

In order to delineate political news content in the media under scrutiny, the following criteria are applied: '[T]he article/story contains a party-political actor, addresses politically relevant subjects or is in some other way related to the campaign, for example appearing as part of the news program's election-extra headline' (Johansson 2008: 184). When these criteria are applied to the morning press in connection with the nine national election campaign in the period 1979–2006, a total of slightly over 26,000 articles emerges; an average of almost 3,000 articles in the morning press are analysed in connection with each election campaign. The corresponding figure for the tabloids is around 7,100. Two election campaigns (1991 and 1994) are missing from the content analysis of the tabloids. Thus, the average number of articles per each election is around a thousand for the tabloid press.

In Johansson's analysis of these data, three aspects pertaining to party leaders are at the centre of attention. First, how frequently do party leaders appear as the central or one of the central actors in articles and news stories? Has there, in other words, been an increasing tendency to centre articles and news coverage on the party leaders? The second aspect deals with the visualization of party leaders, i.e. the extent to which pictures of party leaders are used as illustrations for articles and news stories. Finally, the dramatisation of the election coverage involving party leaders is examined. To what extent does election coverage focus on 'politics as a game', on campaign events, political scandals and opinion-poll reporting rather than on campaign issues, policy content and other substantive questions?

As to the first question, the amount of attention paid to party leaders, data are available for the period 1982–2006[23]. Table 4.1.shows how these figures look for the various election years.

Table 4.1: Party leaders in newspaper election coverage, Sweden 1982–2006. Percentage of articles focusing on party leaders

	1982	1985	1988	1991	1994	1998	2002	2006
Morning press	19	19	16	19	16	16	18	17
Tabloid press	33	30	25	N.A.	N.A.	37	36	36

Source: Johansson 2008: 187

The quarter century covered by the data in Table 4.1 reveals a remarkable degree of stability. The amount of attention paid to party leaders in newspaper reporting has changed little, if at all. Predictably, the tabloid press is characterised by a stronger focus on party leaders than the morning press; this difference may have grown slightly over the years. However, what is remarkable that there is no increase whatsoever in the amount of attention paid to party leaders by the morning press. In this sense, it is simply inaccurate to speak of a growing personalisation in newspaper election coverage.

The role of party leaders in the visualisation of election campaigns is the second aspect covered by Johansson's data. To what extent do party leaders figure centrally in the illustrations used by newspapers in their campaign coverage? Table 4.2 highlights this question.

23 In the 1979 study, actors were measured in a different way, which is why these data are not comparable to the results for 1982-2006.

Table 4.2: *The visualisation of party leaders in newspaper election coverage,* *Sweden 1979–2006. Percentage of party leader pictures of all illustrations*

	1979	1982	1985	1988	1991	1994	1998	2002	2006
Morning press	44	37	42	35	35	34	39	42	43
Tabloid press	43	48	51	42	N.A.	N.A.	62	66	64

Source: Johansson 2008: 188

Again, the morning press displays basically no change at all during the past quarter-century. Roughly 40 per cent of the illustrations tend to portray party leaders, and nothing indicates a clear temporal pattern. As for the tabloids, there seems to be a somewhat stronger tendency to focus on leaders during the last three campaigns, and the difference between the two types of newspapers seems to have increased. Overall, however, it is the stability rather than the change that is striking in these data.

If the amount of attention devoted to party leaders in newspaper campaign coverage is fairly static, what about the kind of attention they receive? Are they today more frequently portrayed in a dramatised context than during earlier years? Are they presented so as to posit them as players in a game, as being involved in scandals or opinion poll 'horse races'? Or do they appear as spokesmen for policies and substantive issues to an equal extent throughout the period studied? Table 4.3 provides answers to these questions.

Table 4.3: *Party leaders in dramatised election coverage, Sweden 1982–2006.* *Percentage of dramatised articles of all articles focusing on party leaders*

	1982	1985	1988	1991	1994	1998	2002	2006
Morning press	29	37	46	43	62	56	60	71
Tabloid press	66	61	65	N.A.	N.A.	68	76	80

Source: Johansson 2008: 189

Comparing Table 4.3 with the two earlier tables reveals a striking difference. While the amount of attention paid to party leaders has not changed very much, party leaders are today presented in a quite different context than a few decades ago. This is particularly true of the morning press; it has basically shifted to the dramatised mode of presentation that has always been prevalent in the tabloid press. Even in the tabloids, however, there has been an increase in dramatised coverage that is today entirely predominant in these newspapers. Overall it is fair to say that when party leaders are present today in leading Swedish newspapers, they appear in a dramatised context. It is not exaggerated to speak of a shift to a new journalistic paradigm during the past two or three decades.

All in all, data on Swedish newspapers convey a dual impression. The amount of attention paid to party leaders is fairly constant over time. The clearly increased dramatisation of election coverage, however, presents party leaders in a context that is quite different from the one typical of the early 1980s.

FINLAND: CAMPAIGN ADVERTISEMENTS

The features of different country's electoral systems largely determine what strategies are feasible and rational in election campaigns. Some systems contain strong incentives for individual candidates to pursue personal campaigns, in certain cases even against candidates of one's own party. The Single Non-transferable Vote system is often said to present such incentives (Carey and Shugart 1995: 429–30). At the opposite extreme we find the closed-list systems, where list position along with the total vote received by the party list decides the electoral fate of candidates. In these systems, those who wish to become elected strongly depend on the endorsement of those who decide the composition of the party list. By the same token, it is the success of the party campaign that determines the chances of individual top-placed candidates to become elected.

The electoral system used for parliamentary elections in Finland, as of the 1958 election, contains considerable incentives for individual candidates to pursue personal campaigns. In this sense, it is clearly a candidate-centred system. The members of the Finnish parliament are chosen from multi-member districts, average district size being around fourteen seats. List totals determine the number of seats won by each party. However, it is the individual votes received by the candidates that determine which of the candidates from each list will be awarded the seats won by the parties in a given district. The Finnish system thus is an example of an open-list PR system; it is the personal popularity of candidates among voters, not a rank-order determined by the party organisations that decides the fortune of individual candidates (Kuusela 1995: 24–9).

While the system encourages prospective representatives to pursue individual campaigns, it does not encourage them to engage in negative campaigning against candidates of their own party. Irrespective of competing personal ambitions, all candidates share the need to maximise the list total received by their party. Should there be strong elements of intraparty mud-slinging among the candidates, this would probably hurt the party list as a whole and consequently diminish the relative chances of all individual candidates to become elected. By the same token, it is in the interest of all candidates that not just their personal campaigns but the party campaign as a whole be conducted in a professional and successful way.

These two elements are clearly present in Finnish parliamentary campaigns. The central party organisations formulate election slogans and platforms that are marketed throughout the country. Party branches carry out party campaigns centring on the candidate lists presented in each electoral district. Meanwhile, individual candidates pursue their personal campaigns in a highly decentralised manner. Central to these campaigns are the support groups that are formed around individual candidates. These groups are not part of the official party organisation and function quite independently of it. They bear the bulk of the financial responsibility for individual campaigns (Ruostetsaari and Mattila 2002: 92–9).

How do Finnish parties and candidates present themselves to the electorate in connection with an election campaign? What is the balance between individual and party campaigns? Have the relative shares of individual and party campaigning changed over time?

In order to provide an answer to these questions, campaign advertisements in Finland's largest daily newspaper *Helsingin Sanomat* were analysed in connection to four parliamentary campaigns from 1962 to 2007. *Helsingin Sanomat* is the only daily newspaper in Finland that has a genuinely nationwide circulation. Its total daily circulation is around 420,000[24]; as the population of Finland is around 5.2 million, this is rather impressive. *Helsingin Sanomat* not only dwarfs its competitors in Finland. It is in fact the largest morning paper in the whole of Scandinavia. From the point of view of Finnish advertisers – political or otherwise – it offers a unique channel to reach a nationwide audience.

A longitudinal analysis is facilitated by the fact that *Helsingin Sanomat* has been remarkably conservative as to its technical format. It has been published in broadsheet format with eight columns per page throughout the period examined. This means that quantitative analyses of content do not run into thorny problems of comparability over time.

All campaign advertisements during the final pre-election week in connection with the 1962, 1975, 1991 and 2007 parliamentary campaigns were included in the study. The final campaign week is the period when advertising peaks. For instance, in connection with the 2007 campaign there was a total of 235 advertisements during the final week. Therefore this method results in empirical material which should be quite sufficient for the present purpose.

The approach is entirely quantitative; qualitative assessments of the content of campaign ads were not undertaken. The ads were divided into three groups:

- *Party advertisements.* These were ads where parties presented themselves either entirely without individual candidates or with the entire slate of candidates, i.e. with all candidates in one or several electoral districts.
- *Other collective advertisements.* In these ads, several candidates rather than a complete list of candidates appeared.
- *Individual advertisements.* These were ads that contained the name, candidate number or picture of a single candidate.

The concrete measure was total advertising space. This was measured as centimetres of column. The height of each advertisement in centimetres times the number of columns was calculated. Table 4.7 shows the results of these measurements.

---

24 See www.levikintarkastus/tilastot/Newspapers10years.pdf

Two main features indicate a fairly clear development over time. The share of pure party ads has declined, and the share of individual ads has grown. However, while the former has gone through a linear decline, the latter displays a jump between 1962 and 1975; from this time onwards, the share of individual campaign ads has been more or less constant. A third feature concerns 'other collective advertisements'. These accounted for very low shares of total advertisements in 1975 and 1991, but became more common again in 2007. Although the figures for 1962 and 2007 are comparable, the ads looked quite different at these two points in time. In the 1962 campaign, a typical advertisement of this kind features representatives of professional or religious groups. In 2007, these ads typically featured two candidates with similar personal images, rather than collective backgrounds or socio-economic characteristics. It seems as if these ads are today used more to mark personal lifestyles than collective identities.

Table 4.7: Three types of campaign advertisements in Helsingin Sanomat in 1962, 1975, 1991 and 2007. Relative shares of advertising volume (per cent)

	1962	1975	1991	2007
Party advertisements	49.0%	40.5%	39.1%	33.7%
Other collective advertisements	7.0%	2.7%	1.6%	8.3%
Individual advertisements	44.0%	56.8%	59.3%	58.0%
Total	100%	100%	100%	100%
Total campaign ads (centimetres of column)	16,994	8805	12,586	12,325

Moreover, it is interesting to note that the total advertising volume was highest in 1962. During the final week of the 1962 campaign, the paper was packed with campaign ads; a decade and a half later, the intensity of advertising had clearly diminished. This does not indicate a shift in the temporal spread of campaign advertising. Instead, two major changes in the conditions for parties and political communication account for this change. The system of public party subsidies, introduced in 1966, enabled parties to reorganise their campaigning in the form of nationwide targeted campaigns carried out by the party organisations reinforced by the influx of public finance. Parties were no longer as dependent on the only major newspaper to reach the general public. Moreover, the introduction of nationwide television in the course of the 1960s made the parties visible to a nationwide audience in an entirely new way. To be sure, outright political advertising on television was not permitted until the 1990s. Still, campaign coverage and party leader debates on television became a central channel for political communication and campaigning on a nationwide scale.

Overall, the development of political advertising in Finland does not point to any dramatic transformation. Still, it is fair to speak of an ongoing individualisation of campaign advertisements over time. In this sense, the Finnish evidence does support the personalisation thesis.

SUMMARY AND CONCLUSIONS

Studies of media and campaign content represent an extremely important part of political analysis. It is here that research meets the political process in the form which is most visible to the ordinary citizen. When it comes to the study of the alleged personalisation of politics, this is even more accurate. To the extent that voters and citizens perceive politics as being primarily connected with individual leaders and candidates, this impression is chiefly conveyed through the media.

At the same time, the comparative study of media content is a demanding field. The systematic analysis of media content is always a cumbersome exercise; comparative studies run easily into linguistic and technical difficulties that may seem insurmountable to an individual researcher.

The present chapter has had to content itself with a more limited number of empirical cases than the previous analyses in the book. Naturally, this means that the possibilities of generalising from this evidence are more restricted. Clearly, contrary findings for the cases scrutinised would have made conclusions impossible to draw.

The three case studies deal with different aspects of the presentation of politics in newspapers. Two of them (Britain and Sweden) reflect the editorial and journalistic choices behind political coverage. The Finnish case tells us something about how parties and politicians wish to present themselves in connection with election campaigns. The three analyses do not result in identical findings; still, they seem to point to developments in roughly the same direction.

As for the quantitative aspect of personalisation, the change seems neither dramatic nor uniform. True, British prime ministers get more coverage in Britain and individual candidates occupy more advertising space in Finland over time. By contrast, Swedish newspapers do not use more space to cover party leaders in connection with election campaigns. More important, however, is the way in which politics is presented. Coverage of political leaders centres on them as individuals more than in the past. They are presented in more familiar terms, their leadership qualities are discussed more and they are seen as players in a political game much more than in the past. Candidates not only appear more than the parties in political advertising. Advertising has also become more personal when several candidates share advertising space. It is more important than in the past to present oneself in terms of image rather than collective social bonds.

In conclusion, although the data presented above do not point to a dramatic transformation, they do offer evidence that goes to support the gist of the personalisation thesis.

conclusion | is there a personalisation of politics?

Adde parvum parvo[1]

NO PERVASIVE TREND, MANY INDICATIONS

Four themes

This book does not support the notion that there has been a clear and pervasive trend towards personalisation among parliamentary democracies. In fact, to the extent that the results presented in the preceding chapters are not mixed they are negative from the point of view of the personalisation thesis. Still, there are reasonably clear differences between the findings of the empirical analyses; looking at different aspects of personalisation leads to partially different conclusions about the phenomenon. In the following, a short summary of the main findings will be presented for the four areas studied empirically. This summary starts with the most positive findings and works its way towards the theme that resulted in the most negative conclusions from the point of view of the personalisation thesis.

- *How politics is presented.* Clearly, the analysis of media content in Chapter 4 resulted in findings that were most positive from the point of view of the thesis. British prime ministers were found to receive increasing media attention; their leadership qualities are discussed more than in the past, and they are referred to in more personal terms than previously. Swedish party leaders are presented in an increasingly dramatised form in connection with campaign coverage in newspapers; on the other hand, the general amount of coverage has remained stable over time. Finnish campaign ads have become more candidate-centred over time; the change is, however, not particularly recent or dramatic.

- *The role of individual candidates.* In those countries where the possibility of choosing between individual candidates has existed for a long time, the relative importance of individual candidates seems to have increased. Sweden, where preferential voting is still fairly new, displays no such tendency. In countries where the electoral system does not allow for intraparty candidate choice no indications of increased candidate saliency were found.

- *Institutions.* In a number of parliamentary democracies, prime ministers, according to expert assessments, have become more influential over time. In a comparable number of cases, however, no similar tendency could be clearly established; even negative cases were found. As for electoral reforms,

---

1   Translation: Add a little to a little and there will be a great heap (Ovid).

a certain tendency towards a greater degree of intraparty candidate choice was discovered among countries with proportional list systems. At the same time, several formerly candidate-centred systems have been reformed in a more party-centred direction.

– *Party leader effects in elections.* No clear evidence was found for the notion that the importance of party leader evaluations for party choice has increased over time. By the same token, voters do not display any tendency to have more intense opinions about party leaders than earlier. Weaker party identification does not foster stronger views on party leaders; in fact it is the other way round. The intensity of party leader evaluations rises rather than declines with age. Party loyalists rather than party switchers have intensive preferences regarding party leaders. In sum, no tendency towards more leader-centred voters can be discerned, and the influx of new voters and the increase in voter volatility can not be expected to alter this picture. These findings essentially support the negative results presented by earlier comparative research.

Much of the empirical analysis must be based on varying evidence from case to case. Moreover, the number of cases was on several points fairly limited. Still, the above conclusions seem justified. From the point of view of the personalisation thesis, it is particularly disheartening that the most positive picture emerged from the analysis where the number of cases was most limited and where strict comparisons were difficult. By the same token, the most systematic evidence – that on party leader effects in elections – led to the most negative conclusions.

Country by country

Conclusions do not only vary depending on the aspect of personalisation that one chooses to study. The development is clearly not uniform from country to country. Now, this conclusion must be drawn with a degree of caution; the countries included in the chapters of this book could not be studied in a uniform manner. Still, the evidence presented does point to differences among the group of stable parliamentary democracies. In the following, the findings for countries included are summarised in a succinct manner. The list starts with those countries where several factors pointed to an increased personalisation. Towards the end, those countries where most indicators were negative will be discussed. The list ends with those countries for which only scanty information was presented.

POSITIVE CASES

Belgium The analysis of expert data on the position of the prime minister pointed to an increase in executive influence; the O'Malley data and the reanalysis of the Belgian case in Poguntke and Webb (2005) gave similar results. Electoral reforms have strengthened the role of individual candidates in Belgian elections. Moreover, there is a steady and clear increase in the incidence of preferential voting in Belgium. These results are supported by van Aalst and Mierlo's (2003) findings about more media focus on individual politicians. It is difficult to say whether there is a common background to these developments. One might, however, point to the fact that there has been a strengthened regionalisation of Belgian politics manifested in particular in the 1993 Constitutional Reform (Derbyshire and Derbyshire 1999: 649). In connection with this reform, the Belgian prime minister's position was strengthened by introducing a constructive vote of no-confidence in Belgian parliamentarism (Fiers and Krouwel 2005: 129). It is likely that these changes have boosted both the role of individual candidates and the position of the executive leader.

Finland. The influence of the Finnish prime minister has grown over time; both the O'Malley data and the reanalysis of Poguntke and Webb point to this change. Finnish voters stress candidate over party more than in the past. Individual electioneering has grown in scope at the expense of collective party advertising. Earlier research (Paloheimo 2005; Pekonen 1995) points to similar trends. Moreover, ongoing research on the Finnish case (Karvonen, forthcoming) corroborates these findings further. Finnish voters attribute party leaders a growing general role when it comes to the electoral fortunes of the parties. Citizens use party leaders as arguments for their personal party choice more often than in the past. The distribution of personal votes among the candidates also points to a growing personalisation of Finnish politics. The new constitution introduced in several steps in the course of the 1990s must be seen as an important cause behind these changes. The constitution stripped the president of her powers vis-à-vis the parliamentary sphere of politics and made the prime minister the most central political actor. The question of who is to be the next prime minister has become increasingly important in Finnish elections (Paloheimo 2003).

Ireland. The O'Malley data point to a trend towards growing prime-ministerial influence, although this trend is not particularly pronounced. Increased vote transfers across party lines point to a decreased party loyalty and an increased importance for individual candidates. Voters increasingly stress candidate over party when it comes to their personal vote choices.

MIXED-POSITIVE CASES

Denmark. According to both sources used in this book, prime-ministerial influence has grown over the years in Denmark. The use of open list nominations by the parties has grown from election to election and is entirely dominant today. By contrast, only around half of the Danish electorate uses the option of casting a preference vote, and this share has remained stable over a long period. Moreover, being one of the countries covered in the *European Voter Database,* Denmark (like the other cases included) displays no growth in party leader effects on party choice among voters.

Israel. This is indeed a mixed case. Rahat and Sheafer's (2007) broadly conceptualised study points to a personalisation of candidate nominations, media coverage and individual activity in the *Knesset.* By contrast, the O'Malley data indicate a decline in prime-ministerial influence, and this impression does not conflict with the results of a re-analysis of Poguntke and Webb. The introduction in 1992 of direct election of prime ministers strongly focused parliamentary elections on party leaders. The repeal of this reform in 2001 once again brought parties as collectives to the fore.

Italy. Prime-ministerial influence has clearly increased in Italy. By contrast, the electoral system, once one of the most candidate-centred systems, has been reformed twice in a party-centred direction. There remains no element of preferential voting in Italy today.

The Netherlands. In the O'Malley database, no trend toward increased prime-ministerial influence can be detected. This is, however, contradicted by the reanalysis of Poguntke and Webb; here, the prime minister's position appears to have been strengthened over time. The electoral system has become slightly more candidate-centred. Moreover, voters' propensity to cast preferential votes has grown, although the political effect of preferential voting is still rather limited. The Netherlands is included in the *European Voter Database*; consequently, negative results can be reported concerning party leader effects on party choice.

New Zealand. The O'Malley database points to increased prime-ministerial influence in New Zealand. The electoral system, by contrast, has become somewhat less candidate-centred.

Sweden. Prime-ministerial influence has grown in Sweden according to both the O'Malley database and the reanalysis of Poguntke and Webb. The introduction of optional preference voting as of the 1998 election gave the electoral system a degree of intraparty candidate choice. Citizens increasingly view this option as principally welcome. However, their propensity to actually use the option has declined, and so has candidate recall among Swedish voters. Media present political leaders in increasingly dramatised forms, but the total amount of attention to party leaders in election campaigns has not grown much. Sweden is included in the *European Voter Database*; consequently, negative results can be reported concerning party leader effects on party choice.

The United Kingdom. There is a trend toward increased prime-ministerial influence in the O'Malley database; this is confirmed by the reanalysis of Poguntke and Webb. Increased media attention is devoted to the prime minister, and his leadership qualities are discussed more often. He is increasingly referred to in personal rather than formal terms. Candidate recall among voters has not increased; in fact it may be in decline. The *European Voter Database* and other empirical sources show that leader effects on citizens' party choices have not increased over time.

MIXED-NEGATIVE CASES

Austria. Prime-ministerial influence has not grown in Austria; in fact the O'Malley database points to a slightly declining trend. The preferential element in the electoral system has been strengthened somewhat, but preferential voting is still a fairly peripheral phenomenon.

Germany. A number of earlier studies have resulted in negative findings (Brettschneider and Gabriel 2003; *European Voter Database*; Kaase 1994; Lessinger and Holtz-Bacha; Poguntke 2005; Schmitt and Ohr 2000; Schulz *et al*

2005). In this study, however, prime- ministerial influence was found to have increased. Moreover, the tendency towards growing ticket-splitting points to a personalisation of constituency voting in Germany.

Malta. In the O'Malley database, Malta displays a negative trend concerning prime-ministerial influence. On the other hand, the 1987 electoral reform has accentuated the need to nominate candidates that will attract first-preference votes.

NEGATIVE CASES

Canada. Prime-ministerial influence has not increased according to either the O'Malley database or the reanalysis of Poguntke and Webb. Johnston (2003) found net leadership effects on voters' party choice to be limited.

Japan. Prime-ministerial influence has not grown in Japan. The electoral reform enacted in 1994 meant that Japan abandoned the most candidate-centred system in existence. The system is still not entirely party-centred but the change was nevertheless clear.

Norway. The O'Malley database points to a negative trend in prime-ministerial influence. Candidate recall has not grown among Norwegian voters. Norway is included in the *European Voter Database*; consequently, negative results can be reported concerning party leader effects on party choice.

CASES BASED ON A SINGLE INDICATOR

There is a trend toward increased prime-ministerial influence in *Australia, Iceland* and *Luxembourg*. For *Portugal*, the O'Malley database and the reanalysis of Poguntke and Webb point in different directions. Prime-ministerial influence displays no growth for *Greece*; for *Spain* the trend is basically negative.

Apples and oranges

It is important to stress what the data on the various dimensions tell us and what they do not. This book is not primarily a comparative study that attempts to explain variation among a selection of cases. Rather, by looking at as many cases and aspects as possible, it tests the idea that there has been a general trend towards more personalisation in parliamentary democracies. This broad empirical ambition has compelled us to treat the cases in different way depending on constitutional features and data availability.

Consequently, when cases are grouped as being positive, mixed or negative this is done with respect to trends over time, not levels of personalisation. The latter are primarily the result of basic constitutional features such as electoral systems. Thus, when, for instance, Belgium is depicted as a positive case and Canada as a negative one, we do not propose that politics is less person-focused in the latter than in the former. Most likely it is the other way round, as constitutional features in Canada make leaders and candidates quite important in parliamentary politics. Still, the evidence presented justifies the conclusion that the trend over time is positive in Belgium but not in Canada. Similarly, other differences in trends are based on sufficient empirical evidence to justify the conclusions presented above.

While there is no general trend toward personalisation in parliamentary democracies, there are many indications that persons have become more prominent in both electoral and executive politics in several countries. It would, however, be incorrect to take this as evidence of the fundamental accuracy of the personalisation thesis. Parliamentary politics is still much more about parties than it is about individual politicians, and this will probably remain so for decades to come.

REFLECTIONS

The kind of mixed results that this study has presented easily provokes the perennial debate about whether the glass is half empty or half full. Surely, both believers and sceptics will find evidence to support their views. Those who hold that the personalisation thesis is fundamentally correct would probably interpret the positive indications presented above as a sign that the process of personalisation is now *under way*. The indications according to that view would be early warnings heralding a pervasive change of political culture.

The sceptic, by contrast, would underline the lack of *general* patterns that support the personalisation thesis. Whatever indications there are in favour of personalisation they can always be questioned with the aid of counter-examples. Moreover, the consistently negative results concerning leader effects on party choice would weigh heavily in the sceptic's scales.

Neither of these viewpoints can be refuted offhand on the basis of the results of this study. The empirical evidence is mixed. True, the lack of general temporal patterns is more troublesome from the point of view of the personalisation thesis than the various positive indications are from the point of view of the sceptic. But the indications are numerous enough not to render the thesis meaningless or completely flawed.

Rather than trying to pass a definite verdict on the status of the thesis, these concluding reflections point to the need for alternative perspectives on the theme. One such theme concerns the relationship between the media and the political process at large. Underlying much of the personalisation thesis is the idea that the way the media, television in particular, treats politics has compelled parties and politicians to act in a certain way. This, in turn, has had effects on how people view politics and form their preferences; ultimately it may even lead to institutional changes. This reasoning rests on the fundamental assumption that the various spheres of politics are strongly interconnected. Important changes in one sphere (media) must necessarily manifest themselves in other spheres (political behaviour, institutions) as well. It can be debated whether this is necessarily the case. For one thing, it is established wisdom in communications studies that while media may have effects on what people think about they more rarely dictate the way people think. Moreover, media never cover all factors that are of importance to people's political beliefs and behaviour. To be sure, media are important as sources of political information for citizens. But citizens continue to be influenced by their backgrounds, socio-economic and cultural characteristics and social networks. Faced with an increasingly homogenised media content they may continue to take political cues from these other sources to a higher degree than one might expect.

A second debatable assumption concerns the relative importance of person and party. In much of the literature on personalisation, it is at least implicitly assumed that if persons mean more, this will automatically mean that the importance of parties is reduced. If this is true, the lack of strong evidence on personalisation may be explained with reference to declining political participation. If the least partisan voters choose not to participate in elections, then non-voting keeps the potentially most person-oriented citizens outside the political sphere. It is quite possible that this is indeed the case, but there is to date no systematic empirical evidence available to corroborate this hypothesis.

It may, however, be incorrect to view person and party as opposites at all. The results in Chapter 4 indicate that strong opinions on party leaders go hand in hand with party identification and party loyalty. It is not necessarily valid that those who have clear party preferences view questions about leaders and candidates as less important. In fact, the data indicate that it may be the other way round. Citizens who think that parties are important also view leaders and candidates as important. Parties, leaders and candidates are about politics, and those citizens who think politics is important think that all these aspects of politics matter. Politically indifferent citizens do not care about parties, but neither do they necessarily care about leaders and candidates.

Finally, one might ask whether the effects of an across the board-personalisation of party behaviour may cancel each other out. If all parties endeavour to present themselves in a uniform manner with personalised campaigns centring on leaders and candidates with exactly the 'right' media image, then voters will have to look for other factors than media image to make up their minds. A uniform campaign behaviour may therefore have the paradoxical effect of augmenting the importance of long-term factors of a structural and substantive nature.

| bibliography

Anckar, D. and Anckar, C. (2000) 'Democracies without Parties', *Comparative Political Studies* 33:2 225–47.

Andeweg, R. B. (2008) 'Netherlands: The Sanctity of Proportionality', in M. Gallagher and P. Mitchell (eds) *The Politics of Electoral Systems*, Oxford: Oxford University Press, 491–510.

Andeweg, R. B. and Irwin, G. A. (2005) *Governance and Politics of the Netherlands*, Basingstoke: Palgrave Macmillan.

Aylott, N. (2005) '"President Persson" – How Did Sweden Get Him?', in T. Poguntke and P. Webb (eds) *The Presidentialization of Politics. A Comparative Study of Modern Democracies*, Oxford: Oxford University Press, 176–98.

Bakvis, H. and Wolinetz, S. B. (2005) 'Canada: Executive Dominance and Presidentialization', in T. Poguntke and P. Webb (eds) *The Presidentialization of Politics. A Comparative Study of Modern Democracies*, Oxford: Oxford University Press, 199–300.

Bartle, J. and Crewe, I. (2003) 'The Impact of Party Leaders in Britain: Strong Assumptions, Weak Evidence', in A. King (ed.) *Leaders' Personalities and the Outcomes of Democratic Elections*, Oxford: Oxford University Press, 70–95.

Bauman, Z. (2001) *The Individualized Society*, Cambridge: Polity Press.

Bengtsson, Å. (2008) *Politiskt deltagande*, Lund: Studentlitteratur.

Bengtsson, Å. and Grönlund, K. (2005) 'Ehdokasvalinta', in Heikki Paloheimo (ed.) *Vaalit ja demokratia Suomessa*, Porvoo: WSOY, 229–51.

Bell, D. (1960) *The End of Ideology. On the Exhaustion of Political Ideas in the Fifties*, New York: The Free Press.

Bennulf, M. and Hedberg,P. (1993) 'Person och parti i massmedierna', in J. Westerståhl (ed.) *Person och parti*, Stockholm: SOU 1993:63, 109–33.

Berglund, F., Holmberg, S., Schmitt, H. and Thomassen, J. (2005) 'Party Identification and Party Choice', in J. Thomassen (ed.) *The European Voter. A Comparative Study of Modern Democracies*, Oxford: Oxford University Press, 106–24.

Bowler S., Farrell, D.M. and Katz, R. (1999) 'Party Cohesion, Party Discipline, and Parliaments', in S. Bowler, D.M Farrell and R. Katz (eds) *Party Discipline and Parliamentary Government*, Columbus: Ohio State University Press, 3–22.

Brettschneider, F. and Gabriel, O. W. (2003) 'The Nonpersonalization of Voting Behavior in Germany', in A. King (ed.) *Leaders' Personalities and the Outcomes of Democratic Elections*, Oxford: Oxford University Press, 127–57.

Calise, M. (2005) 'Presidentialization, Italian Style', in T. Poguntke and P. Webb (eds) *The Presidentialization of Politics. A Comparative Study of Modern Democracies*, Oxford: Oxford University Press, 88–106.

Caprara, G. V. (2007) 'The Personalization of Modern Politics', *European Review* 15:2: 151–64.

Carey, J. M. and Soberg Shugart, M. (1995) 'Incentives to Cultivate a Personal Vote: a Rank Ordering of Electoral Formulas', *Electoral Studies* 14:4: 417–39.

Cox, G. W. (1997) *Making Votes Count. Strategic Coordination in the World's Electoral Systems*, Cambridge: Cambridge University Press.

Curtice, J. (2003) 'Elections as Beauty Contests: Do the Rules Matter?', paper presented at the International Conference on 'Portugal at the Polls', Lisbon, February 2003.

Curtice, J. and Holmberg, S. (2005) 'Party leaders and Party Choice', in J. Thomassen (ed.) *The European Voter. A Comparative Study of Modern Democracies*, Oxford: Oxford University Press, 235–53.

Dalton, R. (2002) 'The Decline of Party Identifications', in R. J. Dalton and M. P. Wattenberg (2002) (eds) *Parties without Partisans. Political Change in Advanced Industrial Democracies*, Oxford: Oxford University Press, 19–36.

Dalton R., McAllister, I. and Wattenberg, M. P. (2002) 'The Consequences of Partisan Dealignment', in R. J. Dalton and M. P. Wattenberg (eds) *Parties without Partisans. Political Change in Advanced Industrial Democracies*, Oxford: Oxford University Press, 37–63.

Dalton, R. J. and M. P. Wattenberg (2002) (eds) *Parties without Partisans. Political Change in Advanced Industrial Democracies*, Oxford: Oxford University Press.

De Winter, L. (2008) 'Belgium: Empowering Voters or Party Elites?', in M. Gallagher and P. Mitchell (eds) *The Politics of Electoral Systems*, Oxford: Oxford University Press, 417–32.

Derbyshire, J. D. and Derbyshire, I. (1999) *Political Systems of the World. Volume 2*, Oxford: Helicon.

D'alimento, Roberto (2008), 'Italy: A Case of Fragmented Bipolarism', In M. Gallagher and P. Mitchell, (Eds) *The Politics of Electoral Systems*, Oxford: Oxford University Press, 253–76.

Elklit, J. (2008) 'Denmark: Simplicity Embedded in Complexity (or is it the Other Way Around)?', in M. Gallagher and P. Mitchell (eds) *The Politics of Electoral Systems*, Oxford: Oxford University Press, 452–71.

Farrell, D. M. (1996) 'Campaign Strategies and Tactics', in L. LeDuc, R. E. Niemi and P. Norris (eds) *Comparing Democracies. Elections and Voting in Global Perspective*, London: Sage Publications, 161–83.

Farrell, D. M. (1997) *Comparing Electoral Systems*, Basingstoke: Macmillan.

Farrell, D. M. and McAllister, I. (2003 'Through a Glass Darkly: Understanding the World of STV', in S. Bowler and B. Grofman (eds) *Elections in Australia, Ireland, and Malta under the Single Transferable Vote. Reflections on an Embedded Institution*, Ann Arbor, Michigan: The University of Michigan Press, 17–36.

Fiers, S. and Krouwel, A. (2005) 'The Low Countries: From 'Prime Minister' to President-Minister', in T. Poguntke and P. Webb (eds) *The Presidentialization of Politics. A Comparative Study of Modern Democracies*, Oxford: Oxford University Press, 128–58.

Foley, M. (1993) *The Rise of the British Presidency*, Manchester: Manchester University Press.

Forschungsgruppe W. (2005) 'Bundestagswahl. Eine Analyse der Wahl vom 18. September 2005', *Berichte der Forschungsgruppe Wahlen e. V., Mannheim Nr 122*.

Gallagher, M. (2008) 'Ireland: The Discreet Charm of PR-STV', in M. Gallagher and P. Mitchell (eds) *The Politics of Electoral Systems*, Oxford: Oxford University Press, 511–32.

Gallagher, M., Laver, M. and Mair, P. (2001) *Representative Government in Modern Europe. Institutions, Parties, and Governments*, New York: McGraw-Hill.

Gallagher, M. and Mitchell, P. (2008) (eds) *The Politics of Electoral Systems*, Oxford: Oxford University Press.

Gidlund, G. (2004) 'Konsten att rigga ett jämlikt val', in Å. Bengtsson and K. Grönlund (eds) *Partier och ansvar*, Stockholm: SNS Förlag, 87–109.

Gschwend, T. (2007) 'Ticket-Splitting and Strategic Voting under Mixed Electoral Rules. Evidence from Germany', *European Journal of Political Research* 46:1–23.

Gschwend, T. and van der Kolk, H. (2006) 'Split Ticket Voting in Mixed-Member Proportional Systems: The Hypothetical Case of the Netherlands', *Acta Politica* 41: 163–79.

Hart, R. P. (1999) *Seducing America. How Television Charms the Modern Voter*, London: Sage Publications.

Hay, C. (2006) 'Constructivist institutionalism', in R.A.W. Rhodes, S. A. Binder and B. A. Rockman (eds) *The Oxford Handbook of Political Institutions*, Oxford: Oxford University Press, 56–74.

Hazan, R. Y. (2005 'The Failure of Presidential Parliamentarism: Constitutional versus Structural Presidentialization In Israel's Parliamentary Democracy', in T. Poguntke and P. Webb (eds) *The Presidentialization of Politics. A Comparative Study of Modern Democracies*, Oxford: Oxford University Press, 289–312.

Heffernan, R.and Webb, P. (2005) 'The British Prime Minister: Much More than "First Among Equals"', in T. Poguntke and P. Webb (eds) *The Presidentialization of Politics. A Comparative Study of Modern Democracies*, Oxford: Oxford University Press, 26–62.

Hessing, R.C. (1985) 'Bij voorkeur: een onderzoek naar het gebruik van voorkeurstemmen', *Acta Politica* 20:2: 157–176.

Holmberg, S. and Möller, T. (1999) 'Premiär för personval', in S. Holmberg and T. Möller (eds) *Premiär för personval*. Stockholm: Elanders Gotab, 7–15.

Holmberg, S. and Oscarsson, H. (2004) *Väljare. Svenskt väljarbeteende under 50 år*, Stockholm: Norstedts juridik.

Inglehart, R. (1971) 'The Silent Revolution in Europe: Intergenerational Change in Postindustrial Societies', *American Political Science Review* 65 (4): 991–1017.

Inglehart, R. (1977) *The Silent Revolution. Changing Values and Political Styles Among Western Publics*, Princeton, N.J.: Princeton University Press.

Inglehart, R. (1990) *Culture Shift in Advanced Industrial Society*, Princeton, N.J.: Princeton University Press.

Inglehart, R. (2007) 'Postmaterialist Values and the Shift from Survival to Self-Expression Values', in R. J. Dalton and H.-D. Klingemann (eds) *The Oxford Handbook of Political Behavior*, Oxford: Oxford University Press, 223–239.

Jennings, M. K. and Niemi, R. G. (1981) *Generations and Politics. A Panel Study of Young Adults and Their Parents*, Princeton, N.J.: Princeton University Press.

Jesse, E. (1988) 'Split-voting in the Federal Republic of Germany: An Analysis of the Federal Elections from 1953 to 1987', *Electoral Studies* 7:2: 109–24.

Johansson, B. (2008) 'Popularized Election Coverage? News Coverage of Swedish Parliamentary Elections 1979–2006', in J. Strömbäck, T. Aalberg and M. Ørsten (eds) *Communicating Politics: Political Communication in the Nordic Countries*, Göteborg: University of Gothenburg, 181–93.

Johnston, R. (2003) 'Prime Ministerial Contenders in Canada', in A. King (ed.) *Leaders' Personalities and the Outcomes of Democratic Elections* Oxford: Oxford University Press, 159–83.

Kaase, M. (1994) 'Is there a Personalization in Politics? Candidates and Voting Behavior in Germany', *International Political Science Review* 15 (3): 211–30.

Karvonen, L. (2002) 'Personval – ingen risk, ingen mirakelmedicin', in H. Hvitfelt and L. Karvonen (eds) *Den personliga politiken*, Sundsvall: Demokratiinstitutet, 24–39.

Karvonen, L. (2004) 'Preferential Voting: Incidence and Effects', *International Political Science Review* 25 (2): 203–26.

Karvonen, L. (forthcoming) 'Politiikan henkilöityminen', in S. Borg and H. Paloheimo (eds) *Vaalit yleisödemokratiassa*, Tampere: Tampere University Press, 95–126.

Keil, S. I. (2003) *Wahlkampfkommunikation in Wahlanzeigen und Wahlprogrammen*, Frankfurt am Main: Peter Lang.

King, A. (2003) 'Conclusions and Implications, in A. King (ed.) *Leaders' Personalities and the Outcomes of Democratic Elections*, Oxford: Oxford University Press, 210–21.

Kirchheimer, O. (1966) 'The Transformation of the Western European Party Systems', in J. LaPalombara and M. Wiener (eds) *Political Parties and Political Development*, Princeton, N.J.: Princeton University Press, 177–200.

Klingemann, H.-D. and Wessels, B. (2001) 'The Political Consequences of Germany's Mixed-Member System: Personalization at the Grass Roots?', in M. Soberg Shugart and M. P. Wattenberg (eds) *Mixed-Member Electoral Systems. The Best of Both Worlds?* Oxford: Oxford University Press, 279–96.

Kuusela, K. (1995) 'The Finnish Electoral System: Basic Features and Developmental Tendencies', in S. Borg and R. Sänkiaho (eds) *The Finnish Voter*, Tampere: The Finnish Political Science Association, 23–44.

Langer, A. I. (2006) *The Politicisation of Private Persona: The Case of Tony Blair in Historical Perspective*, London: London School of Economics and Political Science.

Langer, A. I.(2007) 'A Historical Exploration of the Personalisation of Politics in the Print Media: The British Prime Ministers 1945-1999', *Parliamentary Affairs*, 60(3), 371-387.

Lass, J. (1995) *Vorstellungsbilder über Kanzlerkandidaten. Zur Diskussion um die Personalisierung der Politik*, Wiesbaden: Deutscher Universitäts-Verlag.

Lessinger, E.-M. and Holtz-Bacha, C. (2003) 'Party Electoral Advertising in Germany. Trends in Content and Style from 1957 to 2002', paper for the ECPR General Conference, Marburg September 18–21, 2003.

Lijphart, A. (1986) 'Degrees of Proportionality of Proportional Representation Formulas', in B. Grofman and A. Lijphart (eds) *Electoral Laws and their Political Consequences*, New York: Agathon Press, 170–79.

Lindström, U. (2001) 'From Post-communism to Neo-communism? The Reconstitution of the Party Systems of East-Central Europe', in L. Karvonen and S. Kuhnle (eds) *Party Systems and Voter Alignments Revisited*, London: Routledge, 216–37.

Lobo, M. C. (2008) 'Parties and Leader Effects: Impact of Leaders in the Vote for Different Types of Parties', *Party Politics* 14(3): 281–98.

Lobo, M. C. (2005) 'The Presidentialization of Portuguese Democracy?', in T. Poguntke and P. Webb (eds) *The Presidentialization of Politics. A Comparative Study of Modern Democracies*, Oxford: Oxford University Press, 269–88.

Lundell, K. (2005) *Contextual Determinants of Electoral System Choice. A Macro-Comparative Study 1945–2003*, Åbo: Åbo Akademi University Press.

Mair, P. (2006) 'Cleavages', in R. S. Katz and W. Crotty (eds) *Handbook of Party Politics*, London : SAGE Publications, 370–75.

Manin, B. (1997) *The Principles of Representative Government*, Cambridge: Cambridge University Press.

March J. G. and Olsen, J. P. (2006) 'Elaborating the "New Institutionalism"', in R. A. W. Rhodes, S. A. Binder and B. A. Rockman (eds) *The Oxford Handbook of Political Institutions*, Oxford: Oxford University Press, 3–22.

Marsh, M. (2003) 'Candidate Centered but Party Wrapped: Campaigning in Ireland under STV', in S. Bowler and B. Grofman (eds) *Elections in Australia, Ireland, and Malta under the Single Transferable Vote. Reflections on an Embedded Institution*, Ann Arbor, Michigan: The University of Michigan Press, 114–30.

Marsh, M. (2007) 'Candidates or Parties? Objects of Electoral Change in Ireland', *Party Politics* 13 (4): 500–27.

McAllister, I. (2007) 'The Personalization of Politics', in R. J. Dalton and H.-D. Klingemann (eds) *Oxford Handbook of Political Behavior*, Oxford: Oxford University Press, 571–88.

Mitchell, P. (2008) 'The United Kingdom: Plurality Rule under Siege', in M. Gallagher and P. Mitchell (eds) *The Politics of Electoral Systems*, Oxford: Oxford University Press, 157–84.

Mochmann, I. C. and Zenk-Möltgen, W. (2005) 'The European Voter Data Base', in J. Thomassen (ed.) *The European Voter. A Comparative Study of Modern Democracies*, Oxford: Oxford University Press, 309–12.

Mughan, A. (2000) *Media and the Presidentialization of Parliamentary Elections*, Basingstoke: Palgrave.

Müller, W C. (2008) 'Austria: A Complex Electoral System with Subtle Effects', in M. Gallagher and P. Mitchell (eds) *The Politics of Electoral Systems*, Oxford: Oxford University Press, 397–415.

Narud, H. M. and Valen, H. (2007) *Demokrati og ansvar. Politisk representasjon i et flerpartisystem*, Oslo: N.W. Damm and Søn AS.

Norris, P. (2002) *Democratic Phoenix. Reinventing Political Activism*, Cambridge: Cambridge University Press.

Olsen J. P. (2002) 'Konstitusjonsdebatt og reformer: Europeiske eksperimenter og norsk nøling', *Norsk Statsvitenskapelig Tidsskrift* 2: 91–116.

O'Malley, E. (2007) 'The Power of Prime Ministers: Results of an Expert Survey', *International Political Science Review*, 28 (1): 7–27.

Oscarsson, H. and Holmberg, S. (2008) 'Alliansseger. Redogörelse för 2006 års valundersökning i samarbete mellan Statsvetenskapliga institutionen vid Göteborgs universitet och Statistiska centralbyrån', in *Allmänna valen 2006, Del 4*, Göteborg: Göteborgs Universitet, 187–339.

Paloheimo, H. (2005a) 'Let the Force Be with the Leader – But Who Is the Leader?', in T. Poguntke and P. Webb (eds) *The Presidentialization of Politics. A Comparative Study of Modern Democracies*, Oxford: Oxford University Press, 246–68.

Paloheimo, H. (2005b) 'Puoluevalinnan tilannetekijät', in H. Paloheimo (ed.) *Vaalit ja demokratia Suomessa*. Porvoo: WSOY, 202–28.

Paloheimo, H. (2003) 'The Rising Power of the Prime Minister in Finland', *Scandinavian Political Studies* 26 (3): 219–43.

Pedersen, K. and Knudsen, T. (2005) '"Denmark: Presidentialization in a Consensual Democracy', in T. Poguntke and P. Webb (eds) *The Presidentialization of Politics. A Comparative Study of Modern Democracies*, Oxford: Oxford University Press, 159–75.

Pekonen, K. (1995) 'Finnish Voters and the Personification of Politics', in S. Borg and R. Sänkiaho (eds) *The Finnish Voter*, Tampere: The Finnish Political Science Association, 187–207.

Pesonen, P., Sänkiaho, R. and Borg, S. (1993) *Vaalikansan äänivalta. Tutkimus eduskuntavaaleista ja valitsijakunnasta Suomen poliittisessa järjestelmässä*. Porvoo: WSOY.

Petersson, O., von Beyme, K ., Karvonen, L., Nedelmann, B. and Smith, E. (1999) *Democracy the Swedish Way. Report from the Democratic Audit of Sweden 1999*, Stockholm: SNS Förlag.

Poguntke, T. (2005) 'A Presidentializing Party State? The Federal Republic of Germany', in T. Poguntke and P. Webb (eds) *The Presidentialization of Politics. A Comparative Study of Modern Democracies*, Oxford: Oxford University Press, 63–87.

Poguntke, T. and Webb, P. (2005) 'The Presidentialization of Politics in Democratic Societies: A Framework for Analysis', in T. Poguntke and P. Webb (eds) *The Presidentialization of Politics. A Comparative Study of Modern Democracies*, Oxford: Oxford University Press, 1–25.

Rahat, G. and Sheafer, T. (2007) 'The Personalization(s) of Politics: Israel, 1949–2003', *Political Communication* 24: 65–80.

Rhodes, R.A.W., Binder, S.A. and Rockman, B. A. (eds) (2006) *The Oxford Handbook of Political Institutions*, Oxford: Oxford University Press.

Rihoux, B., Dumont, P. and Dandoy, R. (2001) 'Belgium', *European Journal of Political Research* 40: 254–62.

Ruostetsaari, I. and Mattila, M. (2002) 'Candidate-Centred Campaigns and their Effects in an Open List System. The Case of Finland', in D. M. Farrell and R. Schmitt-Beck (eds) *Do Political Campaigns Matter? Campaign Effects in Elections and Referendums*, London: Routledge, 92–107.

Saalfeld, T. (2008) 'Germany: Stability and Strategy in a Mixed-Member Proportional System', in M. Gallagher and P. Mitchell (eds) *The Politics of Electoral Systems*, Oxford: Oxford University Press, 209–29.

Schmitt, H. and Ohr, D. (2000) 'Are Party Leaders Becoming More Important in German Elections? Leader Effects on the Vote in Germany', paper for APSA, Washington, D.C., August 31 – September 3, 2000.

Schmitt-Becker, R. and Farrell, D. M. (2002) 'Studying Political Campaigns and Their Effects', in D. M. Farrell and R. Schmitt-Beck (eds) *Do Political Campaigns Matter? Campaign Effects in Elections and Referendums*, London: Routledge, 1–21.

Schulz, W., Zeh, R. and Quiring, O. (2005) 'Voters in a Changing Media Environment: A Data-Based Retrospective on Consequences of Media Change in Germany', *European Journal of Communication* 20 (1): 55–88.

Shugart, M. S. (2001) 'Electoral "Efficiency" and the Move to Mixed-Member Systems', *Electoral Studies* 20: 173–93.

Sinnott, R. (1995) *Irish Voters Decide. Voting Behaviour in Elections and Referendums since 1918*, Manchester: Manchester University Press.

SOU 1993:21 'Ökat personal. Betänkande av personvalskommittén', Stockholm 1993: Norstedts tryckeri AB.

Strandberg, K. (2006) *Parties, Candidates and Citizens On-Line. Studies of Politics on the Internet*, Åbo: Åbo Akademi University Press.

Swanson, D. L. and Mancini, P. (1996a) 'Patterns of Modern Electoral Campaigning and Their Consequences', in D. L. Swanson and P. Mancini (eds) *Politics, Media, and Modern Democracy. An International Study of Innovations in Electoral Campaigning and Their Consequences*, Westport, Connecticut: Praeger, 247–76.

Swanson, D. L. and Mancini, P. (1996b) 'Politics, Media, and Modern Democracy: Introduction', in D. L. Swanson and P. Mancini (eds) *Politics, media, and Modern Democracy. An International Study of Innovations in Electoral Campaigning and Their Consequences*, Westport, Connecticut: Praeger, 1–28.

Thomsen, S. R. and Elklit, J. (2007) 'Hvad betyder de personlige stemmer for partiernes tilslutning?', in J. G. Andersen, J. Andersen, O. Borre, K. M. Hansen and H. J. Nielsen (eds) *Det nye politiske landskab. Folketingsvalget 2005 i perspektiv*, Århus: Academica, 307–34.

Topf, R. (1998) 'Beyond Electoral Participation', in H.-D. Klingemann and D. Fuchs (eds) *Citizens and the State*, Oxford: Oxford University Press, 52–91.

Törnudd, K. (1968) *The Electoral System of Finland*, London: Hugh Evelyn.

Trantas, G., Zagoriti, P., Bergman, T., Müller, W. C. and Strøm, K. (2006) 'Greece: "Rationalizing" Constitutional Powers in a Post-dictatorial Country', in K. Strøm, W. C. Müller and T. Bergman (eds) *Delegation and Accountability in Parliamentary Democracies*, Oxford: Oxford University Press, 376–98.

van Aalst, P. and van Mierlo, K. (2003) 'Politiek als One-Man-Show? Over de rol van kranten in de personalisering van de politiek', *Res Publica* 4: 579–602.

van Biesen, I. and Hopkin, J. (2005) 'The Presidentialization of Spanish Democracy: Sources of Prime Ministerial Power in Post-Franco Spain', in T. Poguntke and P. Webb (eds) *The Presidentialization of Politics. A Comparative Study of Modern Democracies*, Oxford: Oxford University Press, 107–27.

Wass, H. (2008) 'Generations and Turnout. The Generational Effect in Electoral Participation in Finland', *Acta Politica 35, Department of Political Science, University of Helsinki*.

Wattenberg, M. (1991) *The Rise of Candidate-Centered Politics: Presidential Elections of the 1980s*, Cambridge, Massachusetts: Harvard University Press.

Wauters, B. (2003) 'Het gebruik van voorkeurstemmen bij de federale parlementsverkiezingen van 18 mei 2003', *Res Publica* 2(3): 401–28.

Weber, M. (1957) *The Theory of Social and Economic Organization*, New York: Oxford University Press.

Webb, P. (2002) 'Political Parties in Advanced Industrial Democracies', in P. Webb, D. Farrell and I. Holliday (eds) *Political Parties in Advanced Industrial Democracies*, Oxford: Oxford University Press, 1–15.

Webb, P. and Poguntke, T. (2005) 'The Presidentialization of Contemporary Democratic Politics: Evidence, Causes, and Consequences', in T. Poguntke and P. Webb (eds) *The Presidentialization of Politics. A Comparative Study of Modern Democracies*, Oxford: Oxford University Press, 336–56.

DATABASES

Electoral Systems and the Personal Vote. http://dss.ucsd.edu/~jwjohnso/espv.html

European Voter Database. www.gesis.org/en/services/data/survey-data/election-studies/international-election-studies/the-european-voter/?0=

FSD1260. Parliamentary Election Survey 2003 [electronic database]. Gallup Finland [data collection]. Finnish Social Science Data Archive [distribution]. www.fsd.uta.fi/english/index.html

FSD2269. Parliamentary Election Survey 2007 [electronic database]. Gallup Finland [data collection]. Finnish Social Science Data Archive [distribution]. www.fsd.uta.fi/english/index.html

Irish Opinion Poll Archive, www.tcd.ie/Political_Science/IOPA/index.php

Prime Ministerial Power. http://webpages.dcu.ie/~omalle/

index